Parrot Fire Kris Northern

"Rather than zoom into the fractal you can zoom into the edge of it and continually find the same pattern repeating itself much like the shoreline of a lake viewed from a plane." – **Kris Northern**

Investigations
IN NUMBER, DATA, AND SPACE®

Editorial offices: Glenview, Illinois • Parsippany, New Jersey • New York, New York
Sales offices: Boston, Massachusetts • Duluth, Georgia
Glenview, Illinois • Coppell, Texas • Sacramento, California • Mesa, Arizona

The Investigations curriculum was developed by TERC, Cambridge, MA.

This material is based on work supported by the National Science Foundation ("NSF") under Grant No. ESI-0095450. Any opinions, findings, and conclusions or recommendations expressed in this material are those of the author(s) and do not necessarily reflect the views of the National Science Foundation.

ISBN: 0-328-24066-4
ISBN: 978-0-328-24066-1

2 3 4 5 6 7 8 9 10-V031-15 14 13 12 11 10 09 08 07

GRADE 5 CONTENTS

Parrot Fire Kris Northern

"Rather than zoom into the fractal you can zoom into the edge of it and continually find the same pattern repeating itself much like the shoreline of a lake viewed from a plane." – **Kris Northern**

Investigations

IN NUMBER, DATA, AND SPACE®

Number Puzzles and Multiple Towers

Investigation 3

UNIT 1 CONTENTS

Number Puzzles: 1 Clue (page 1 of 2)

For each number puzzle, follow these steps.

a. Find two numbers that fit each clue.

b. Draw rectangles, and label the dimensions to show that your numbers fit the clue.

c. List other numbers that also fit the clue.

1. This number of tiles will make a rectangle that is 2 tiles wide.

Number: _____   Number: _____

Rectangle: Rectangle:

What other numbers fit this clue? _____

2. This number of tiles will make a rectangle that is 5 tiles wide.

Number: _____   Number: _____

Rectangle: Rectangle:

What other numbers fit this clue? _____

3. This number of tiles will make only one rectangle.

Number: _____   Number: _____

Rectangle: Rectangle:

What other numbers fit this clue? _____

Number Puzzles: 1 Clue (page 2 of 2)

4. | This number of tiles will make a square. |

Number: _____   Number: _____
Rectangle: Rectangle:

What other numbers fit this clue? _____

5. There are some numbers that can be made into only one rectangle (Problem 3). Find all of these numbers up to 50.

6. There are some numbers that can make a square (Problem 4). Find all of these numbers up to 100.

Factors and Multiples

NOTE Students find factors and multiples of 2-digit numbers.

SMH **18–19**

1. List all of the factors of 42.

2. List five multiples of 42.

3. Explain the difference between a *factor* and a *multiple*.

Ongoing Review

4. Which number is **not** a factor of 36?

   A. 4   **B.** 8   **C.** 9   **D.** 12

5. Which number **is** a multiple of 36?

   A. 200   **B.** 108   **C.** 76   **D.** 48

Seeing Number Dot Patterns

Look at each picture in different ways. Write equations to show different ways to multiply that you can see in the picture.

1.  Example $5 \times 3 \times 2 = 30$

_____

_____

_____

2.

_____

_____

3.

_____

_____

Number Puzzles: 2 Clues (page 1 of 2)

For each number puzzle, follow these steps.

a. Find two numbers that fit both clues.

b. Draw rectangles, and label the dimensions to show that your numbers fit both clues.

c. List other numbers that also fit both clues.

1.

| This number of tiles will make a rectangle that is 2 tiles wide. | and | This number of tiles will make a rectangle that is 4 tiles wide. |

Numbers: _____   _____

Rectangles:

What other numbers fit this clue? _____

Number Puzzles: 2 Clues (page 2 of 2)

2.

| This number of tiles will make a rectangle that is 3 tiles wide. | and | This number of tiles will make a rectangle that is 4 tiles wide. |

Numbers: _____ _____

Rectangles:

What other numbers fit this clue? _____

3.

| This number of tiles will make a rectangle that is 20 tiles wide. | and | This number of tiles will make a rectangle that is 25 tiles wide. |

Numbers: _____ _____

Rectangles:

What other numbers fit this clue? _____

Computation Practice: Adding Two Ways

Solve this problem in two different ways. Be sure to show how you got your answer.

NOTE Students practice strategies for solving addition problems. They work on efficiency and flexibility by solving the same problem in two different ways.

SMH 8–9

$$1{,}018 + 879 = \underline{\hspace{2cm}}$$

First way:

Second way:

Number Puzzles Recording Sheet

Check off each puzzle you solve. Record your answer.

Investigation 1 Number Puzzles

✓	Puzzle	Answer
	1	
	2	
	3	
	4	
	5	
	6	
	7	
	8★	
	9★	
	10★	
	11★	
	12★	
	13	
	14	

Multiplication Combinations 1

Multiply each number in the first column of the table with the number at the top. For example, the answer for the first blank space in Table A is 14, which is 2 × 7. Circle any combinations you do not know immediately, and record them on *Student Activity Book* page 10.

> **NOTE** Fifth-grade students are expected to know their multiplication combinations (facts). This page helps students determine whether they remember their combinations and identify any combinations they still need to practice.
>
> **SMH** 25–29

Table A	
× 7	
2	14
6	
8	
3	
10	
11	
7	
12	
4	
9	
5	

Table B	
× 8	
2	
9	
4	
11	
8	
10	
6	
5	
3	
12	
7	

Table C	
× 6	
10	
4	
2	
8	
3	
6	
9	
5	
12	
11	
7	

Table D	
× 9	
5	
2	
12	
4	
10	
7	
3	
6	
11	
8	
9	

Multiplication Combinations
Recording Sheet

> **NOTE** Fifth-grade students are expected to know their multiplication combinations (facts). On this sheet, students write any combination they still need to practice and a clue to help them learn it. An example is shown on the left.
>
> **25–29**

Example: $\underline{\ 7\ } \times \underline{\ 9\ } = \underline{\ 63\ }$ and $\underline{\ 9\ } \times \underline{\ 7\ } = \underline{\ 63\ }$

Clue: $\underline{\ 7 \times 10 = 70 \qquad\qquad 70 - 7 = 63\ }$

_____ × _____ = _____ and _____ × _____ = _____

Clue: _____

_____ × _____ = _____ and _____ × _____ = _____

Clue: _____

_____ × _____ = _____ and _____ × _____ = _____

Clue: _____

_____ × _____ = _____ and _____ × _____ = _____

Clue: _____

_____ × _____ = _____ and _____ × _____ = _____

Clue: _____

_____ × _____ = _____ and _____ × _____ = _____

Clue: _____

Number Puzzles

1. Solve the following number puzzle.

> **NOTE** Students solve and create number puzzles to help learn about the composition of numbers.
>
> **SMH** 21–22

Clue 1	Clue 2
This number is a factor of 48.	This number is even.
Clue 3	**Clue 4**
This number is a multiple of 6.	The sum of the digits of this number equals 3.

What number is it? _____

2. Make up your own number puzzle.

Clue 1	Clue 2
Clue 3	**Clue 4**

The number is _____.

Ongoing Review

3. Which number fits the following clues?

   Clue 1 This number is even.
   Clue 2 This number is a factor of 54.

   A. 3   **B.** 6   **C.** 9   **D.** 12

Multiplying to Make 18 and 180

1. Find all the multiplication combinations you can for these two numbers, using whole numbers. Start by multiplying two factors. Then find ways to multiply with more than two factors.

18	180

2. How did finding the ways to multiply with two numbers help you find ways to multiply with more than two numbers?

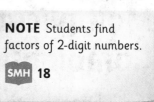

Factors of 2-Digit Numbers

NOTE Students find factors of 2-digit numbers.

SMH 18

1. Find all of the factors of 36.

2. Find all of the factors of 72.

3. How are the factors of 36 related to the factors of 72?

Ongoing Review

4. Which number is **not** a factor of 124?

A. 31   **B.** 12   **C.** 4   **D.** 2

Multiplication Combinations 2

> **NOTE** Fifth-grade students are expected to know their multiplication combinations (facts). This page helps students determine whether they remember their combinations and identify any combinations they still need to practice.
>
> **SMH** 25–29

Multiply each number in the first column of the table with the number at the top. For example, find the product of 3 × 7 for the first blank space in Table A.

In Tables C and D, write a number at the top for a group of combinations you need to practice.

Circle any combinations you do not know immediately, and record them on *Student Activity Book* page 10 or on M30 that your teacher will give you.

Table A			Table B			Table C			Table D		
	× 7			× 8			× ____			× ____	
3			2			10			5		
6			7			4			2		
9			3			2			12		
2			5			8			4		
4			6			3			10		
10			10			6			7		
8			8			9			3		
12			11			5			6		
5			12			12			11		
7			4			11			8		
11			9			7			9		

All of the Ways to Multiply

Find all of the ways to multiply to make each product, using whole numbers. First, find the combinations with two factors, and then find ways to multiply with more than two factors.

1.

12	**120**

2.

21	**210**

Factors of 3-Digit Numbers

NOTE Students find factors of 3-digit numbers.

SMH 18

1. Find all of the factors of 100.

2. Find all of the factors of 200.

3. Did you use the factors of 100 to find the factors of 200? If so, how?

Ongoing Review

4. Which number is **not** a factor of 150?

   A. 3   **B.** 15   **C.** 75   **D.** 125

Multiplication Combinations 3

Multiply each number in the first column of the table with the number at the top. For example, find the product of 9 × 6 for the first blank space in Table A.

In Tables C and D, write a number at the top for a group of combinations you need to practice.

Circle any combinations you do not know immediately, and record them on *Student Activity Book* page 10 or on M30 which your teacher will give you.

> **NOTE** Fifth-grade students are expected to know their multiplication combinations (facts). This page helps students determine whether they remember their combinations and identify any combinations they still need to practice.
>
> **SMH** 25–29

Table A		Table B		Table C		Table D	
× 6		× 8		× ___		× ___	
9		4		10		12	
4		5		5		9	
7		3		12		8	
5		2		7		7	
8		6		4		2	
3		10		2		11	
12		7		8		3	
2		12		6		4	
11		8		3		10	
6		4		12		5	
10		9		9		6	

Multiplication Combinations
for 120, 180, and 210 (page 1 of 2)

Think about these questions and give examples from your
work on pages 12 and 15 to explain your answers.

1. How did the multiplication combinations you wrote for
   12, 18, and 21 help you find some combinations for
   120, 180, and 210? Give examples.

2. How did you figure out ways to multiply with three or
   more factors?

3. How did you know that you found all the possible
   multiplication combinations for each number?

Multiplication Combinations
for 120, 180, and 210 (page 2 of 2)

4. Write the longest multiplication combination you found for each of these numbers.

120

180

210

5. Look at the numbers above. Is it possible to find a different way to multiply with the same number of factors as what you wrote in Problem 4? (This does not include multiplying the same factors in a different order.)

_____

How do you know?

Daily Practice

Factors and Multiples of 3-Digit Numbers

> **NOTE** Students find factors and multiples of 3-digit numbers.
>
> **SMH** 18–19

1. Find all of the factors of 150.

2. List five multiples of 150.

Ongoing Review

3. Which multiplication combination equals 300?

    A. $2 \times 30 \times 6$ **C.** $15 \times 2 \times 10$

    B. $10 \times 6 \times 20$ **D.** $2 \times 3 \times 15$

Multiplication Combinations 4

In the top blank in each table, write a number for a group of combinations you need to practice. Then multiply each number in the first column of the table by the number at the top.

Circle any combinations you do not know immediately, and record them on *Student Activity Book* page 10 or on M30 which your teacher will give you.

> **NOTE** Fifth-grade students are expected to know their multiplication combinations (facts). This page helps students determine whether they remember their combinations and identify any combinations they still need to practice.
>
> **SMH** 25–29

Table A	
× ____	
2	
4	
6	
8	
10	
12	
3	
5	
7	
9	
11	

Table B	
× ____	
11	
2	
10	
5	
9	
6	
7	
8	
3	
12	
4	

Table C	
× ____	
9	
11	
8	
6	
10	
4	
12	
7	
5	
3	
2	

Table D	
× ____	
5	
9	
2	
12	
3	
8	
6	
4	
7	
11	
10	

Multiplying to Make 60 and 90

Find as many ways as you can to multiply whole numbers to make each product.

> **NOTE** Students find multiplication combinations with two factors and with more than two factors for 60 and for 90.
>
> **SMH** 23–24

1. Multiplying to make 60

Ways to multiply with two factors:	Ways to multiply with more than two factors:

2. Multiplying to make 90

Ways to multiply with two factors:	Ways to multiply with more than two factors:

Ongoing Review

3. Which multiplication combination equals 150?

   A. $10 \times 5 \times 10$ **C.** $25 \times 2 \times 3$

   B. $75 \times 2 \times 10$ **D.** $10 \times 5 \times 5$

Multiplication Combinations 5

In the top blank in each table, write a number for a group of combinations you need to practice. Then multiply each number in the first column of the table by the number at the top.

Circle any combinations you do not know immediately, and record them on *Student Activity Book* page 10 or on M30 which your teacher will give you.

> **NOTE** Fifth-grade students are expected to know their multiplication combinations (facts). This homework helps students determine whether they remember their combinations and identify any combinations they still need to practice.
>
> **SMH** 25–29

Table A	
× _____	
4	
8	
6	
2	
9	
12	
3	
5	
7	
11	
10	

Table B	
× _____	
6	
10	
2	
11	
4	
12	
9	
8	
5	
7	
3	

Table C	
× _____	
5	
7	
8	
3	
9	
4	
11	
6	
12	
10	
2	

Table D	
× _____	
3	
5	
2	
6	
9	
10	
4	
11	
12	
8	
7	

Multiplying 2-Digit Numbers

Solve these problems and show your work.

NOTE Students multiply two 2-digit numbers.

SMH 30–32

1. 26 × 12

2. 18 × 34

Ongoing Review

3. 12 × 18 = _____

    A. more than 400   **C.** about 200

    B. about 300   **D.** less than 100

Factors of 50 and 72

Find as many ways as you can to multiply using whole numbers to make each product.

NOTE Students practice finding multiplication combinations with two factors and with more than two factors for 50 and 72.

SMH **23–24**

1. Multiplying to Make 50

Ways to multiply with two factors:	Ways to multiply with more than two factors:

2. Multiplying to Make 72

Ways to multiply with two factors:	Ways to multiply with more than two factors:

Solving Multiplication Problems

Choose three of these problems to solve. Show your work.
Use clear and concise notation.

After you have solved the problems, pick at least one of
your solutions and use a representation to show how you
solved it.

27×19 42×32 76×8 82×56 65×14

Multiplying Two Ways

NOTE Students multiply a 2-digit number in two different ways.

SMH 30–32

1. Solve this problem in two different ways. Show each solution clearly.

$$26 \times 19 = \underline{\hspace{2cm}}$$

First way:

Second way:

Ongoing Review

2. $6 \times 3 \times 10 \times 2 =$ _____

   A. 120   **B.** 300   **C.** 360   **D.** 630

Multiplication Practice

Solve the problems below. Show your solution clearly.

NOTE In class, students are solving multiplication problems. They are using story contexts and representations to help them solve the problems and explain their solutions. As they solve the problems below, ask them what part of the problem they have solved and what part they still need to solve.

 SMH 30–32

1. 24 × 15

2. 49
   × 9
   ‾‾‾‾

3. 36 × 25

Multiplication Compare Recording Sheet

After you have played a few rounds of *Multiplication Compare*, complete this sheet.

Place a <, >, or = in the box between the problems.

1. Your problem: Partner's problem:

_____ × _____   ☐   _____ × _____

How did you decide whose product
is greater? Explain your reasoning.

2. Your problem: Partner's problem:

_____ × _____   ☐   _____ × _____

How did you decide whose product
is greater? Explain your reasoning.

3. Your problem: Partner's problem:

_____ × _____   ☐   _____ × _____

How did you decide whose product
is greater? Explain your reasoning.

More Multiplying Two Ways

NOTE Students multiply 2-digit numbers in two different ways.

SMH **30–32**

1. Solve this problem in two different ways. Show each solution clearly.

$$36 \times 26 = \underline{\hspace{2cm}}$$

First way:

Second way:

Circle the problem that has the greater product. Circle both if they are equal.

2. 6×40 5×50

3. 40×20 200×4

4. 300×20 100×40

Which Is Greater?

Circle the problem that has the greater product, and write < or > between the problems. (Remember that the wide-open part of the symbol is toward the greater number and the point is toward the smaller one.) Put = between the problems if the products are equal.

In the space to the right of the problems, write how you decided which answer is greater.

NOTE Students have been solving multiplication problems that involve multiples of 10, such as 20, 30, 40, 100, 200, and so on.

SMH 30–32

1. 20×50 ☐ 30×40	
2. 7×80 ☐ 70×8	
3. 200×40 ☐ 100×80	
4. 50×60 ☐ 40×70	
5. 300×7 ☐ 30×70	

Multiplication Cluster Problems

1. Solve these problems.

$10 \times 12 =$ _____ $20 \times 12 =$ _____

$20 \times 10 =$ _____ $8 \times 10 =$ _____

$28 \times 2 =$ _____

Now solve $28 \times 12 =$ _____.

How did you solve it?

2. Solve these problems.

$35 \times 10 =$ _____ $10 \times 25 =$ _____

$35 \times 20 =$ _____ $20 \times 25 =$ _____

$30 \times 25 =$ _____

Now solve $35 \times 25 =$ _____.

How did you solve it?

3. Solve these problems.

$10 \times 21 =$ _____ $20 \times 20 =$ _____

$20 \times 21 =$ _____ $7 \times 20 =$ _____

$5 \times 21 =$ _____

Now solve $27 \times 21 =$ _____.

How did you solve it?

4. Solve these problems.

$100 \times 7 =$ _____ $15 \times 7 =$ _____

$40 \times 7 =$ _____ $150 \times 7 =$ _____

Now solve $146 \times 7 =$ _____.

How did you solve it?

Problems Involving Teams

Solve the problems below. Your work should be clear enough so that anyone looking at it will know how you solved the problem.

1. There are 37 teams and 28 students on each team. How many students are there?

2. There are 68 teams at the soccer tournament. Each team has 16 players. How many soccer players are at the tournament?

3. There are 49 teams in the youth football league. Each team has 28 players. How many football players are there?

4. There are 57 teams entered in the relay race for Field Day. Each team has 32 people. How many people are entered in the relay race?

5. There are 44 teams and 35 people on each team. How many people are on teams?

Daily Practice

More Multiplying 2-Digit Numbers

NOTE Students multiply 2-digit numbers.

SMH 30–32

Solve these problems. Show each solution clearly.

1. 48 × 34

2. 28 × 21

Ongoing Review

3. Is the product of 32 × 28

    A. more than 1,000?

    B. between 500 and 1,000?

    C. between 100 and 500?

    D. less than 100?

Many Ways to Multiply

Find all of the ways to multiply to make each product.
First, find the ways with two factors, and then find ways
to multiply with more than two factors.

NOTE Students find
ways to multiply to
make each product.

 23–24

1. 144

2. 300

More Multiplication Cluster Problems

1. Solve these problems.

$10 \times 26 =$ _____ $30 \times 2 =$ _____

$20 \times 26 =$ _____ $30 \times 6 =$ _____

$30 \times 26 =$ _____

$5 \times 26 =$ _____

Now solve $36 \times 26 =$ _____.

How did you solve it?

2. Solve these problems.

$49 \times 10 =$ _____ $40 \times 7 =$ _____

$49 \times 20 =$ _____ $40 \times 60 =$ _____

$9 \times 60 =$ _____

Now solve $49 \times 67 =$ _____.

How did you solve it?

3. Solve these problems.

$10 \times 15 =$ _____ $125 \times 10 =$ _____

$20 \times 15 =$ _____ $125 \times 5 =$ _____

$100 \times 15 =$ _____

Now solve $125 \times 15 =$ _____.

How did you solve it?

4. Solve these problems.

$60 \times 80 =$ _____ $60 \times 90 =$ _____

$2 \times 9 =$ _____ $2 \times 90 =$ _____

$2 \times 80 =$ _____

Now solve $62 \times 89 =$ _____.

How did you solve it?

Computation Practice: Subtracting Two Ways

NOTE Students practice strategies for solving subtraction problems. They work on efficiency and flexibility by solving the same problem in two different ways.

SMH 10–13

1. Solve this problem in two different ways.
   Be sure to show how you got your answer.

$$\$30.50 - \$17.79 = \underline{\hspace{2cm}}$$

First way:

Second way:

Starter Problems (page 1 of 2)

1. Solve these problems.

   a. $30 \times 20 =$ _____ **b.** $40 \times 20 =$ _____ **c.** $39 \times 10 =$ _____

   Now choose one of the problems above as the first
   step to solve this problem. Show your solution.

   $39 \times 26 =$ _____

2. Solve these problems.

   a. $33 \times 100 =$ _____ **b.** $30 \times 50 =$ _____ **c.** $10 \times 55 =$ _____

   Now choose one of the problems above as the first
   step to solve this problem. Show your solution.

   $33 \times 55 =$ _____

Starter Problems (page 2 of 2)

3. Solve these problems.

a. $47 \times 10 =$ _____ **b.** $40 \times 30 =$ _____ **c.** $10 \times 36 =$ _____

Now choose one of the problems above as the first step to solve this problem. Show your solution.

$47 \times 36 =$ _____

4. Solve these problems.

a. $6 \times 15 =$ _____ **b.** $100 \times 15 =$ _____ **c.** $106 \times 10 =$ _____

Now choose one of the problems above as the first step to solve this problem. Show your solution.

$106 \times 15 =$ _____

Computation Practice: Addition and Subtraction

Solve the problems below. Show your solutions, using clear and concise notation.

> **NOTE** Students practice addition and subtraction problems.
>
> **SMH** 8–9, 10–13

1.   536
     +247
	2. 724
	     −243

3. 551 + 463 = _____	**4.** 620 −125
5. _____ + 840 = 1,600	**6.** _____ − _____ = 350
7. _____ + _____ = 1,250	**8.** 800 − _____ = 275

More Starter Problems (page 1 of 2)

Finish solving the problems with the first step that is given.
Then solve the same problem in your own way. Record
both of your solutions, using clear and concise notation.

1. $68 \times 75 = $ _____

   a. Start with 60×70.

   b. Solve 68×75 another way.

2. $98 \times 36 = $ _____

   a. Start with 100×36.

   b. Solve 98×36 another way.

Number Puzzles and Multiple Towers

More Starter Problems (page 2 of 2)

3. $16 \times 128 =$ _____

   a. Start with 4×128.

   b. Solve 16×128 another way.

4. $207 \times 46 =$ _____

   a. Start with 207×10.

   b. Solve 207×46 another way.

"How Far?" Problems

Solve the following problems, and explain how you found the distance between the numbers.

NOTE Students use addition and subtraction to solve problems.

SMH 8–9, 10–13

1. How far is it from 752 to 1,000?

2. How far is it from 619 to 2,000?

3. How far is it from 1,345 to 3,000?

4. How far is it from 4,658 to 5,000?

Dividing by 2-Digit Numbers

> **NOTE** Students solve a division problem, show their solution, and write a story problem.
>
> SMH **38–39**

1. Solve the following problem. Show your solution clearly.

    $162 \div 12$

2. Write a story problem that represents $162 \div 12$.

3. What is the answer to your story problem?

Ongoing Review

4. Is the product of 19×45

   A. about 500?

   C. about 1,500?

   B. about 1,000?

   D. about 2,000?

Solve in Two Ways

Solve this problem in two different ways.
Show your work clearly.

$$46 \times 37 = \underline{\hspace{2cm}}$$

First way:

Second way:

Problems about Multiples of 21 (page 1 of 2)

Use the multiple tower for 21 or your list of multiples of 21 to help you with these problems. Be sure to use your answers to the earlier problems to help you with the later problems.

1. $10 \times 21 = $ _____

2. $105 \div 21 = $ _____

3. $315 \div $ _____ $ = 21$

4. _____ $\times 21 = 420$

5. $5 \times 21 = $ _____

6. $210 \div 21 = $ _____

7. $15 \times 21 = $ _____

Problems about Multiples of 21 (page 2 of 2)

8. _____ $\times$ 21 = 630

9. 945 $\div$ _____ = 21

10. 441 $\div$ 21 = _____

11. Write and solve two division problems using multiples of 21.

Story Problems: Reading a Long Book

NOTE Students practice solving addition and subtraction problems in a story problem context.

SMH 8–9, 10–13

1. Noemi borrowed a new book from the library. At 1,000 pages, it is the longest book she has ever tried to read! The first day, she read 115 pages. How many more pages does she have to read to reach the end?

2. During the next week, Noemi read 388 pages. How many pages has she read altogether?

3. At the end of 2 weeks, Noemi had read 816 pages. How many pages does she have left to finish the book?

Solving 315 ÷ 21

NOTE Students have been solving division problems. Students should think about what multiplication combinations they know that can help them solve this problem.

 38–39

1. Write a story problem for 315 ÷ 21.

2. Solve 315 ÷ 21.

Division Problems

Solve the following problems. Make sure anyone looking at your work can tell how you solved the problem.

1. Write a word problem for $21\overline{)252}$ and solve it.

2. There are 415 biographies in the school library. If each shelf holds 27 books, how many shelves are completely filled? How many books are left?

3. Write a word problem for the equation $525 \div 21 =$ _____. Then solve it.

4. There are 748 students eating lunch in the cafeteria at school. The same number of students is sitting at each of 22 tables. How many students are sitting at each table?

Name _____   Date _____

Daily Practice

Story Problems: School Supplies

NOTE Students practice solving addition and subtraction problems in a story problem context.

SMH 8–9, 10–13

1. Mr. Mancillas had $200 to spend on art supplies. He spent $103.80 on drawing paper and $86.35 on paint brushes.

b. How much money did he have left after he bought the art supplies?

2. Mrs. Kim had $300 to spend on science materials. She spent $77.49 on thermometers and $219.99 on a microscope.

b. How much money did she have left after she bought the science materials?

Numbers Off the Tower

Use the multiple tower to solve these problems. Make sure that your work is clear enough that someone looking at it will know how you solved the problem.

1. $1{,}344 \div 21 =$ _____

2. _____ $\times\ 21 = 1{,}512$

3. $21\overline{)1{,}275}$

4. $2{,}121 \div$ _____ $= 21$

5. Write two of your own problems, using multiples not on the tower. Solve the problems.

Story Problems: Stamp Collection

NOTE Students practice solving addition and subtraction problems in a story problem context.

SMH **8–9, 10–13**

1. Helena has a collection of stamps. She has 734 South American stamps and 555 African stamps.

   a. How many stamps does Helena have?

   b. How many more stamps does she need to have 1,500 altogether?

2. Kaetwan also has a stamp collection. He has 839 stamps from Africa and 472 stamps from North America.

   a. How many stamps does Kaetwan have?

   b. How many more stamps does he need to have 1,500 altogether?

3. How many more stamps does Kaetwan have in his collection than Helena has in her collection?

Multiple Tower for 15
(page 1 of 2)

> **NOTE** Students have been using a list of multiples (similar to the strip on the right side of this page) to solve division problems.
>
> **SMH** 20

1. Complete the multiple tower at the right, and stop when you get to 480.

2. How many 15s are in 450? Solve without counting and show how you did it.

3. The 10th, 20th, and 30th multiples of 15 are 150, 300, and 450. What are the 40th and 50th multiples of 15? How do you know?

90
75
60
45
30
15

Multiple Tower for 15 (page 2 of 2)

4. Jean has 270 flowers and 15 vases. If she puts an equal number of flowers in each vase, how many flowers will go in each one?

5. Solve $15\overline{)645}$. Show your solution.

Division Cluster Problems (page 1 of 2)

1. Solve these problems.

$30 \div 15 =$ _____

$60 \div 15 =$ _____

$150 \div 15 =$ _____

Now solve $190 \div 15 =$ _____.

How did you solve it?

2. Solve these problems.

$10 \times 18 =$ _____

$5 \times 18 =$ _____

Now solve $18\overline{)252}$.

How did you solve it?

3. Solve these problems.

$75 \times 2 =$ _____

$75 \times 4 =$ _____

$75 \times 6 =$ _____

Now solve $525 \div 75 =$ _____.

How did you solve it?

4. Solve these problems.

$160 \div 16 =$ _____

$80 \div 16 =$ _____

$320 \div 16 =$ _____

Now solve $450 \div 16 =$ _____.

How did you solve it?

Division Cluster Problems (page 2 of 2)

5. Solve these problems.

$10 \times 21 =$ _____

$20 \times 21 =$ _____

$30 \times 21 =$ _____

Now solve $21\overline{)700}$.

How did you solve it?

6. Solve these problems.

$270 \div 27 =$ _____

$540 \div 27 =$ _____

Now solve $594 \div 27 =$ _____.

How did you solve it?

7. Solve these problems.

$10 \times 25 =$ _____

$20 \times 25 =$ _____

$30 \times 25 =$ _____

$40 \times 25 =$ _____

Now solve $982 \div 25 =$ _____.

How did you solve it?

8. Solve these problems.

$100 \div 25 =$ _____

$1,000 \div 25 =$ _____

$2,000 \div 25 =$ _____

Now solve $2,300 \div 25 =$ _____.

How did you solve it?

Division

Solve the following problems. Show your solutions clearly.

NOTE Students solve division problems and show their solutions.

SMH **38–39**

1. $288 \div 16 =$ _____

2. $600 \div 15 =$ _____

Ongoing Review

3. $900 \div 20 =$ _____

A. 450   **B.** 45   **C.** 40   **D.** 20

Division Practice

Solve these division problems. Your notation should be clear enough so that anyone looking at your work will know how you solved the problem.

NOTE Students practice solving division problems.

SMH **38–39**

1. There are 432 magazines in the library. Each shelf holds 12 magazines. How many shelves hold magazines?

2. There are 8 schools in town, and 408 books were donated to the school libraries. If the books are distributed evenly, how many books will each library receive?

3. $850 \div 25 =$ _____

4. $935 \div 21 =$ _____

Division Compare Recording Sheet

After you have played a few rounds of *Division Compare*,
complete this sheet.

Place a <, >, or = in the box between the problems.

1. Your problem: Partner's problem:

_____ ÷ _____ ☐ _____ ÷ _____

How did you decide whose problem has the greater
quotient? Explain your reasoning.

2. Your problem: Partner's problem:

_____ ÷ _____ ☐ _____ ÷ _____

How did you decide whose problem has the greater
quotient? Explain your reasoning.

3. Your problem: Partner's problem:

_____ ÷ _____ ☐ _____ ÷ _____

How did you decide whose problem has the greater
quotient? Explain your reasoning.

Problems about *Division Compare*

Two people were playing *Division Compare*. These are the problems they had to solve as a result of the cards they picked. Place a $<$, $>$, or $=$ sign between the problems, and explain how you decided which problem has the greater quotient.

1. Player A: Player B:

$800 \div 400$ ☐ $900 \div 10$

Explanation:

2. Player A: Player B:

$200 \div 50$ ☐ $90 \div 50$

Explanation:

3. Player A: Player B:

$600 \div 70$ ☐ $400 \div 20$

Explanation:

4. Player A: Player B:

$600 \div 40$ ☐ $70 \div 10$

Explanation:

Solving Division Problems (page 1 of 2)

Solve each of the following problems. Be sure to answer the question posed by the story context.

1. There are 406 students in Grades 3, 4, and 5. There are 14 classrooms, and each classroom has the same number of students. How many students are in each classroom?

2. Melissa has 880 baseball cards that she wants to store in envelopes. If each envelope holds 35 cards, how many envelopes does she need?

3. Joel collects stamps and has 1,200 international stamps that he wants to put in an album. Each page holds 45 stamps. How many pages will he use?

Solving Division Problems (page 2 of 2)

Write a word problem for each division problem.
Your word problem should end in a question. Solve
the problem and answer the question.

4. $807 \div 7 =$ _____

5. $945 \div 21 =$ _____

6. $620 \div 42 =$ _____

Story Problems: Selling Fruit

> **NOTE** Students practice solving addition and subtraction problems in a story problem context.
>
> **SMH** 8–9, 10–13

1. On Monday, a grocery store received a shipment of 1,000 apples. The apples were quite tasty, and the store sold 346 of them that day. How many apples were left to sell?

2. On Wednesday, the store received a shipment of 1,200 oranges. The store sold 263 oranges that day. How many oranges were left to sell?

3. On Saturday, the store received a shipment of 2,000 mangos. The store sold 415 mangos on Saturday and 680 mangos on Sunday.

    a. How many mangos did the store sell on the weekend (Saturday and Sunday)?

    b. How many mangos were left to sell?

Practicing Multiplication and Division (page 1 of 2)

NOTE Students continue to practice solving multiplication and division problems.

SMH 14

Solve the following problems. Make sure that anyone looking at your work can tell how you solved the problem.

1. There are 64 teams at the basketball tournament. Each team has 12 players. How many players are at the basketball tournament?

2. Write a word problem for $35\overline{)490}$ and solve it.

3. Michael has 275 baseball cards that he wants to store in envelopes. If he puts 25 cards in each envelope, how many envelopes does he need?

Practicing Multiplication and Division (page 2 of 2)

4. There are 118 rows in the auditorium. If 29 people sit in each row, how many people are in the auditorium?

5. Mrs. Garcia teaches fifth grade. She has 720 pattern blocks and 24 plastic containers. If she wants to divide the pattern blocks evenly, how many will she put in each container?

6. Write a word problem for 13 × 42 and show your solution.

Coin Jars

NOTE Students solve problems about combinations of coins.

 63

Find two different solutions to each of these problems.

1. Duante has a coin jar full of pennies, dimes, nickels, and quarters. Most of the coins in his jar are pennies. He knows that there is $7.00 in his coin jar. What combination of coins could be in Duante's coin jar that would equal $7.00?

First Solution	Second Solution

2. Ursula also has a coin jar. There are only two kinds of coins in her coin jar. She knows that there is $3.75 in her jar. What combination of coins could be in Ursula's coin jar that would equal $3.75?

First Solution	Second Solution

Multiple Towers and Filmmaking

Use multiple towers to help you find the answers.

NOTE Students solve real-world problems involving the math content of this unit.

 20

1.  This is a single frame of movie film. In the early years of motion pictures, filmmakers used 16 frames per second to film a silent movie.

How many frames of film are there in 12 seconds of a silent movie? Explain how you found the answer.

2.  In today's motion pictures, filmmakers use 24 frames per second.

How many frames of film are there in 12 seconds of a modern movie? _____ 25 seconds? _____

1 minute? _____

At 24 frames per second, how many seconds would it take to show 504 frames? _____

3.  Many cartoons show 24 separate pictures per second.

How many pictures does a cartoonist need to draw for a 30-second cartoon? _____

4. Suppose that a silent movie is run on modern equipment at 24 frames per second. Would the action in the movie appear to be in slow motion or speeded up? Why do you think so?

"Rather than zoom into the fractal you can zoom into the edge of it and continually find the same pattern repeating itself much like the shoreline of a lake viewed from a plane." – **Kris Northern**

Investigations
IN NUMBER, DATA, AND SPACE®

Prisms and Pyramids

Investigation 1

How Many Cubes? (page 1 of 2)

How many cubes fit in each box? First, determine the number of cubes without building the box. Then build a box and use cubes to check. Check your first answer with your actual answer before going on to the next box.

Think about a way you could find the number of cubes that would fit in any box without building it.

	Pattern	Box	First Answer	Actual Answer
1. Box 1		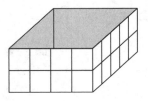	_____	_____
2. Box 2	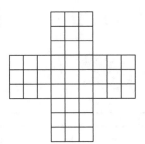	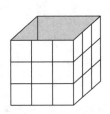	_____	_____
3. Box 3	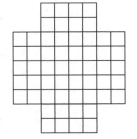		_____	_____

Prisms and Pyramids

How Many Cubes? (page 2 of 2)

	Pattern	Box	First Answer	Actual Answer
4.	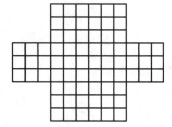		_____	_____
5.		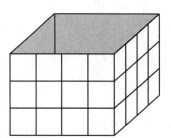	_____	_____

6. The bottom of the box is 4 units by 5 units. The box is 3 units high.

_____ _____

A Strategy for Finding Volume

Describe a way to find how many cubes will fit
in a rectangular box without building the box and
filling it with cubes. Your method should work for any
box, whether you start with a box pattern, a picture
of the box, or a description of the box in words.

Will They Fit?

These sugar cubes are Amy's birthday gift to her horse, Henrietta.

> **NOTE** Students figure out which of three box patterns to use for packaging some sugar cubes. Students should show the sugar cubes with blocks or other cubes if they have difficulty answering the questions.
>
> **SMH** 106–107

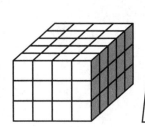 

You're Invited to Henrietta's Birthday Party

1. How many sugar cubes are in the top layer? _____

2. How many layers of sugar cubes are there? _____

3. How many sugar cubes are there in all? _____

4. Which of these patterns should Amy use to make a box for the sugar cubes?

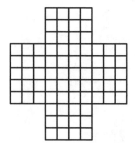 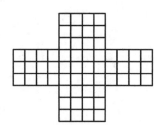 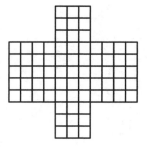

Ongoing Review

5. My number is less than 32. My number is a multiple of 3. The digits of my number add up to 6. What is my number?

   A. 150   **B.** 42   **C.** 24   **D.** 18

Multiplication Practice

Solve each problem in two different ways.
Show your work clearly.

NOTE Students develop flexibility while solving multiplication problems.

 SMH **30–32**

1.   27 × 62 = _____

First way:	Second way:

2.   54 × 48 = _____

First way:	Second way:

Volume of Boxes (page 1 of 2)

What is the volume (the number of cubes that fit) of each box? Determine the number of cubes first, and then build the box and use cubes to check.

	Pattern	**Picture**	**First Answer**	**Actual Answer**

1.

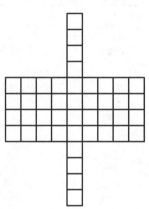

_____ _____

2.

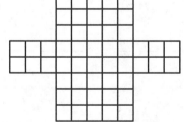   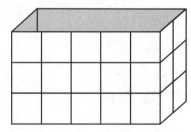

_____ _____

Volume of Boxes (page 2 of 2)

For Problems 3–5, draw the pattern of the box on three-quarter-inch grid paper.

	First Answer	**Actual Answer**

3. 3 by 4 by 3   _____   _____

4.

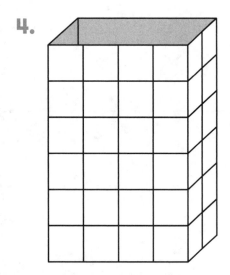

_____   _____

5. The bottom of the box is 5 units by 6 units. The box is 2 units high.   _____   _____

What Should We Do with the Extras?

NOTE Students practice solving division problems and interpreting remainders in story contexts.

SMH 37

Solve each of the following problems. Show your work clearly. Be sure to answer the question posed by the story context.

1. Alicia and her father went food shopping. Oranges were priced at $0.27 each. Alicia and her father have $5.00. How many oranges can they buy?

   Division Equation: _____ ÷ _____ = _____

   Answer: _____

2. Milk cartons come in crates of 24. How many crates does a school need to order to serve milk to 400 students?

   Division Equation: _____ ÷ _____ = _____

   Answer: _____

3. Sixteen people are going to share 200 crackers evenly. How many crackers does each person get?

   Division Equation: _____ ÷ _____ = _____

   Answer: _____

More Boxes

NOTE Students determine how many cubes fit in each of the pictured boxes.

SMH 106–107

1. How many cubes will fit?

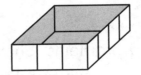

2. How many cubes will fit?

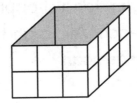

3. How many cubes will fit?

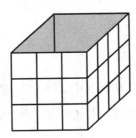

4. How many cubes will fit?

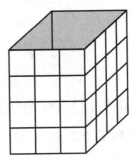

Doubling the Number of Cubes

Answer these questions. Use grid paper, cubes, and anything else that helps you solve the problem.

1. You have a box that is 2 by 3 by 5. How many cubes does it hold? How do you know?

2. The factory wants you to build a box that will hold twice as many cubes. What are the dimensions of a box that contains two times as many cubes as a box that is 2 by 3 by 5? Write the dimensions and explain how you found the answer.

3. Draw the design for the new box below or on graph paper.

Challenge: See how many boxes you can find that will hold two times as many cubes as a 2 by 3 by 5 box. Record each of the dimensions.

Multiplication Practice: Solve Two Ways

NOTE Students develop flexibility while solving multiplication problems.

SMH 30–32

Solve each problem in two different ways.
Show your work clearly.

1. $42 \times 88 =$ _____

First way:	Second way:

2. $57 \times 38 =$ _____

First way:	Second way:

The Symphony (page 1 of 2)

Solve each of the following problems. Show your work clearly. Be sure to answer the question posed by the story context.

Yesterday was Fifth Graders Day at the Civic Symphony Orchestra.

NOTE Students practice solving multiplication and division problems in story contexts.

SMH 30–32, 38–39

1. The Greendale School District sent 11 buses. There were 45 students on each bus. How many fifth graders came from the Greendale schools?

2. The Greendale fifth graders sat in the balcony at Symphony Hall. 15 students sat in each row. How many rows did they fill?

The Symphony (page 2 of 2)

3. The Springfield School District sent 14 buses. There were 55 students on each bus. How many fifth graders came from the Springfield schools?

4. The Springfield fifth graders sat on the first floor at Symphony Hall. 35 students sat in each row. How many rows did they fill?

How Many Packages in Box 1?

   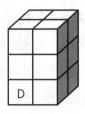 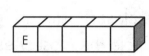

These five packages will be shipped in Box 1. The box is packed with only one type of package at a time. How many of Package A will fit in Box 1? (You may not break apart packages.) How many of Package B will fit in Box 1? Package C? D? E?

First, determine how many packages will fit in the box. Then make the box and check your first answer. Use the pattern on "How Many Packages? Pattern for Box 1" (two pages). Record your answer both before and after filling the box.

Box 1

4 by 6 cubes on the bottom
and 3 cubes high

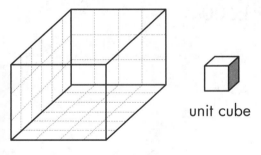

unit cube

How many of each package
will fit in Box 1?

	First Answer	Actual Answer
A	_____	_____
B	_____	_____
C	_____	_____
D	_____	_____
E	_____	_____

Closest Estimate (page 1 of 2)

NOTE Students practice strategies for estimating products.

SMH 30–32

Each problem below has a choice of three estimates. Which one do you think is closest? Choose the closest estimate *without* solving the problem. Circle the closest estimate. Then write about why you think this estimate is the closest.

1. The closest estimate for 84 × 19 is _____.

      1,600   1,800   2,000

I think this is the closest because:

2. The closest estimate for 49 × 28 is _____.

      1,400   1,500   1,600

I think this is the closest because:

Closest Estimate (page 2 of 2)

3. The closest estimate for 16×128 is _____.

  1,500   2,000   2,500

I think this is the closest because:

4. The closest estimate for 207×46 is _____.

  6,000   8,000   10,000

I think this is the closest because:

5. Choose one or more of the problems above and, on
a separate sheet of paper, solve it to get an exact
answer. Show your solution with equations. Did you
choose the closest estimate?

Factors of 160 and 240

Using whole numbers, find all the ways to multiply to make each product. First, find the ways with two numbers, and then find ways to multiply with more than two numbers.

> **NOTE** Students practice finding multiplication expressions with two numbers and with more than two numbers for 160 and 240.
>
> **SMH** 23–24

1. Multiplying to make 160

Ways to multiply with two numbers: Example: 16×10	Ways to multiply with more than two numbers: Example: $2 \times 8 \times 10$

2. Multiplying to make 240

Ways to multiply with two numbers:	Ways to multiply with more than two numbers:

Finding Volume

Find the volume of each rectangular prism described below.
Show how you found the answer. Pick two of the prisms,
and draw the design for the box on centimeter grid paper.

1. The prism is 6 units by 4 units by 5 units.

2. The prism is 3 units by 10 units by 3 units.

3. The prism is 5 units by 7 units by 4 units.

4. The prism is 10 units by 4 units by 6 units.

5. The prism is 8 units by 9 units by 4 units.

Changing Dimensions (page 1 of 2)

Solve the following problems using any material that will help you find the answer.

1. Find the dimensions of a box that will hold **twice** as many cubes as a box that is 2 by 6 by 4.

   Volume of original box: _____

   Volume of new box: _____

   Dimensions of new box: _____

   Explain how you found the dimensions of the new box.

2. Find the dimensions of a box that will hold **twice** as many cubes as a box that is 4 by 2 by 9.

   Volume of original box: _____

   Volume of new box: _____

   Dimensions of new box: _____

   Explain how you found the dimensions of the new box.

3. Find the dimensions of a box that will hold **twice** as many cubes as a box that is 4 by 5 by 6.

   Volume of original box: _____

   Volume of new box: _____

   Dimensions of new box: _____

   Explain how you found the dimensions of the new box.

Changing Dimensions (page 2 of 2)

Now, the packaging factory wants you to find boxes that hold **half** as many cubes.

4. Find the dimensions of a box that will hold **half** as many cubes as a box that is 2 by 8 by 10.

Volume of original box: _____

Volume of new box: _____

Dimensions of new box: _____

Explain how you found the dimensions of the new box.

5. Find the dimensions of a box that will hold **half** as many cubes as a box that is 6 by 5 by 6.

Volume of original box: _____

Volume of new box: _____

Dimensions of new box: _____

Explain how you found the dimensions of the new box.

6. Describe a general strategy to find dimensions for any rectangular box whose volume is **doubled.** Your strategy should work for any box.

Solving Division Problems

NOTE Students practice solving division problems.

 SMH 38–39

1. **a.** Write a story problem that represents $252 \div 14$.

   b. Solve $252 \div 14$. Show your solution clearly.

2. **a.** Write a story problem that represents $23\overline{)575}$.

   b. Solve $23\overline{)575}$. Show your solution clearly.

Prisms and Pyramids

How Many Packages in Box 2?

Now work with Packages A, D, and E and Box 2. How
many of each package will fit in this box? Determine the
answer before building, and then make the box and check.
Record your first answer and the actual answer below.

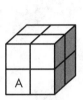
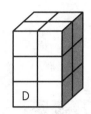
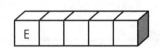

Box 2

4 by 6 cubes on the bottom
and 5 cubes high

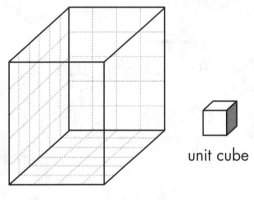

unit cube

How many of each package
will fit in Box 2?

	First Answer	Actual Answer
A	_____	_____
D	_____	_____
E	_____	_____

Multiplication Clusters

Use the cluster problems to help you solve each problem. Circle the problems in the cluster you use.

> **NOTE** Students have been breaking larger products into smaller parts. For example, 48×24 can be broken into 40×24 and 8×24. There are many different ways to combine the smaller products. Ask students to show you more than one way for one or two problems.
>
> **SMH** 35

1. $48 \times 24 =$ _____

2×24	5×24	10×24	20×24
4×24	8×24	40×24	50×24

2. $73 \times 31 =$ _____

2×31	3×31	10×31	20×31
7×31	8×31	70×31	80×31

3. $58 \times 17 =$ _____

2×17	10×17	5×17	50×17
4×17	8×17	20×17	60×17

Ongoing Review

4. Solve 42×8.

A. 3,216   **B.** 1,632   **C.** 336   **D.** 316

Double the Number of Cubes (page 1 of 2)

> **NOTE** Students find the volume of a box (how many cubes fit inside) and create another box to hold twice as many cubes.
>
> SMH 108

Solve the following problems.

1. You have a box that is 2 by 3 by 4.
How many cubes does it hold?
How do you know?

2. The factory wants you to build a box that will hold
twice as many cubes. What are the dimensions of
a box that contains two times as many cubes as a
box that is 2 by 3 by 4? Write the dimensions
and explain how you found the answer.

Double the Number of Cubes (page 2 of 2)

3. Draw the design for the new box below or on graph paper.

Challenge: See how many boxes you can find that will hold two times as many cubes as a 2 by 3 by 4 box. Record each of the dimensions.

Design a Box

Design a single open box so that packages of size A completely fill your box, packages of size B completely fill your box, packages of size C completely fill your box, and packages of size D completely fill your box. Be prepared to convince the class that your solution is correct.

   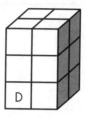

When you have made a box and tested that it works, record its dimensions.

Dimensions: _____

Challenge: Design a single open box that can be completely filled with Package A, B, C, or D, and also with Package E. What are the dimensions of this box? Can you find other boxes that will work?

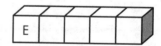

Dimensions: _____

Multiplication Starter Problems

NOTE Students practice flexibility with solving multiplication problems.

 **SMH** 30–32

Solve each problem two ways, using the first steps listed below. Show your work clearly.

1.   49 × 25 = _____

| Start by solving 50 × 25. | Start by solving 40 × 25. |

2.   115 × 28 = _____

| Start by solving 100 × 28. | Start by solving 115 × 10. |

Solving Division Problems (page 1 of 2)

NOTE Students practice solving division problems.

SMH 38–39

Write a story problem that represents each division expression. Then solve the problem.

1. **a.** Write a story problem that represents 528 ÷ 24.

b. Solve 528 ÷ 24. Show your solution clearly.

Solving Division Problems (page 2 of 2)

2. **a.** Write a story problem that represents $16\overline{)368}$.

   b. Solve $16\overline{)368}$. Show your solution clearly.

Factors of 120 and 210

Find all the ways to multiply to make each product, using whole numbers. First, find the ways with two numbers, and then find ways to multiply with more than two numbers.

> **NOTE** Students practice finding multiplication expressions with two numbers and with more than two numbers for 120 and 210.
>
> **SMH** 23–24

1. Multiplying to make 120

Ways to multiply with two numbers: Example: 12×10	Ways to multiply with more than two numbers: Example: $2 \times 6 \times 10$

2. Multiplying to make 210

Ways to multiply with two numbers:	Ways to multiply with more than two numbers:

Division

Solve each division problem below. Then write
the related multiplication combination.

NOTE Students review
division problems that are
related to the multiplication
combinations they know.

SMH 14, 25–29

Division Problem	Multiplication Combination
1. $72 \div 8 =$ _____	_____ × _____ = _____
2. $66 \div 6 =$ _____	_____ × _____ = _____
3. $56 \div 7 =$ _____	_____ × _____ = _____
4. $96 \div 12 =$ _____	_____ × _____ = _____
5. $77 \div 11 =$ _____	_____ × _____ = _____
6. $54 \div 9 =$ _____	_____ × _____ = _____
7. $108 \div 12 =$ _____	_____ × _____ = _____
8. $49 \div 7 =$ _____	_____ × _____ = _____

Large and Small Hunt

In each row, circle the largest product or quotient.
Then underline the smallest.

NOTE Students estimate the answers to multiplication and division problems.

SMH 30–32, 38–39

1.	46 × 77	67 × 51	39 × 86
2.	23 × 97	36 × 58	69 × 33
3.	468 ÷ 26	68 ÷ 34	114 ÷ 6
4.	225 ÷ 15	905 ÷ 5	224 ÷ 16

Ongoing Review

5. Which multiplication fact is related to 72 ÷ 9 = 8?

    A. 8 × 9 = 72   **C.** 7 × 10 = 70

    B. 72 ÷ 8 = 9   **D.** 80 ÷ 8 = 10

Measurements of Volume

NOTE Students, with the aid of an adult/adults, find volumes for common household items.

SMH 109–110

Look in and around your home for any recorded measurements of volume. Look on household items (refrigerators and freezers), in manuals, on other written materials (a water bill), or on any item that might have a measurement of volume recorded on it (the trunk space of a car).

Record any measurements that are given in **cubic** units. Write down both the **number** of cubic units and the **kind** of cubic units used.

This Is Where My Measurement Was Found	Number of Cubic Units	Kind of Cubic Units

Containers from Home

We will soon be comparing the volumes of different household containers. Please find 3 or 4 clean, empty containers at home to bring to school. The recycling bin is a good place to look.

The containers should have sealed edges with no small openings so that sand does not leak out. As a guideline for size, the containers should fit together comfortably in a paper lunch bag.

Volleyball

Solve each of the following problems. Show your
work clearly. Be sure to answer the question posed
by the story context.

> **NOTE** Students practice
> solving multiplication
> problems in story contexts.
>
> **30–32**

1. At a volleyball tournament, there are 23 teams and
   each team has 14 players. How many players are at
   the tournament?

2. There is seating at the tournament so that each of the
   23 teams can invite 30 fans to cheer for them. How
   many seats are at the tournament?

3. Each team is allowed to spend $55 on food and drinks
   for the tournament. How much money do the 23 teams
   spend altogether?

4. At next year's tournament, the number of teams will
   double to 46 teams with 14 players on each. How
   many players will attend that tournament?

Boxes for Centimeter Cubes (page 1 of 2)

You have a box that is 3 centimeters by
4 centimeters by 6 centimeters.

1. How many centimeter cubes does it hold? _____
   How do you know?

Find two boxes that will hold **twice** as many
centimeter cubes as the box above.

2. **a.** What are the dimensions of each new box?

   Dimensions of first box: _____

   Dimensions of second box: _____

   b. Explain how you found the answers.

3. Draw the designs for the new boxes on centimeter
   grid paper.

Boxes for Centimeter Cubes (page 2 of 2)

Find two boxes that will hold **half** as many
centimeter cubes as the 3 centimeters by
4 centimeters by 6 centimeters box.

4. **a.** What are the dimensions of each new box?

Dimensions of first box: _____

Dimensions of second box: _____

b. Explain how you found the answers.

5. Draw the designs for the new boxes on centimeter
grid paper.

Challenge: Find a box that will hold **four** times as many
centimeter cubes as the 3 centimeters by 4 centimeters by
6 centimeters box. Write the dimensions of the new box
and explain how you found your answer.

Double Design

1. Who won the contest? Explain your answer.

NOTE Students have been discussing ways to describe the dimensions of a box. Some ways are 6 wide, 2 long, 3 high; $6 \times 2 \times 3$; and 6 by 2 by 3. As your child judges the boxes in this contest, encourage him or her to compare the new dimensions with those of the current box to help judge how much each new box will hold.

SMH 108

Contest:

Design a box that will hold twice as many cubes as our current box.

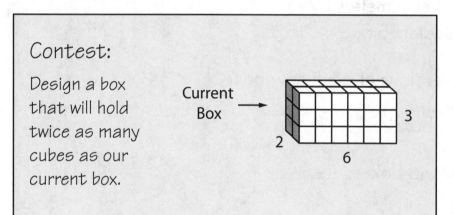

Current Box →

2

6

3

My box is $6 \times 4 \times 3$.

My box is 6 by 8 by 6.

My box is 12 wide by 8 long by 6 high.

Victoria   Ralph   Sandy

AND THE WINNER IS _____!

Ongoing Review

2. There are 56 notebooks being shared equally by a class of 28 students. Which division sentence shows this situation?

A. $56 \div 28 = 2$ **C.** $28 \div 56 = 2$

B. $56 - 28 = 28$ **D.** $28 \div 2 = 14$

Pairs of Solids

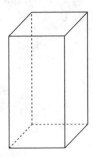 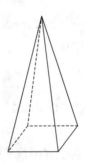

Pair 1

rectangular
prism A

rectangular
pyramid B

Pair 2

cylinder C

cone D

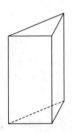 

Pair 3

triangular
prism E

triangular
pyramid F

Pair 4

cylinder G

cone H

Pair 5

rectangular
prism I

rectangular
pyramid J

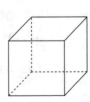

Pair 6

rectangular
prism I

rectangular
pyramid K

Coins

NOTE Students practice solving division problems in a money context.

Solve the following problems. Make sure that anyone looking at your work can tell how you solved the problem.

Alex, Nora, and Felix each won $27.75 in a contest.

1. Alex decided to collect his money all in quarters. How many quarters did he get?

2. Nora chose to get her prize all in dimes and nickels. Show 2 different possible combinations of dimes and nickels that would total $27.75.

    First way: Second way:

3. Felix wanted to collect his money in quarters, dimes, and nickels. Show 2 different possible combinations of quarters, dimes, and nickels that would total $27.75.

    First way: Second way:

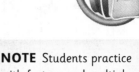

Guess My Number Puzzles

Solve the following problems. If you find only one number that fits, explain how you know that it is the only one. If you find more than one number that fits, explain how you know that you have found all of the possibilities.

NOTE Students practice with factors and multiples of numbers.

 18, 19

1. My number is a multiple of 15.
   My number is also a multiple of 10.
   My number is greater than 100.
   My number is less than 200.

2. My number is a multiple of 150.
   9 is a factor of my number.
   My number has 3 digits.
   The sum of the digits in my number is 9.

3. My number is square.
   My number is even.
   My number has 3 digits.
   3 is a factor of my number.

Picture It

Picture 1-centimeter cubes along the
width, length, and height of the box
below. Write the dimensions of the box.

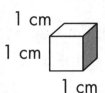

1 cm
1 cm
1 cm

> **NOTE** In class, students
> found the number of cubic
> centimeters needed to fill
> a box. A cube that is 1
> centimeter on each edge
> holds a cubic centimeter.
>
> **SMH** 106–107

1.

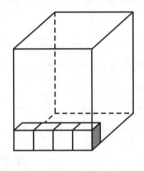 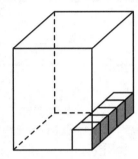 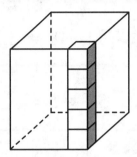

_____ cm wide   _____ cm long   _____ cm high

Figure out how many cubic centimeters will fit in the box.
Tell how you did it.

Ongoing Review

2. Use the cluster problems
to find 47×60.

   A. 2,240

   B. 2,640

   C. 2,820

   D. 3,060

$7 \times 60 = 420$
$4 \times 60 = 240$
$40 \times 60 = 2,400$
$47 \times 60 = ?$

Division Practice

Solve each division problem below. Then write the related multiplication combination.

NOTE Students review division problems that are related to known multiplication combinations.

 SMH 14, 25–29

Division Problem	Multiplication Combination
1. 54 ÷ 9 = _____	_____ × _____ = _____
2. 55 ÷ 5 = _____	_____ × _____ = _____
3. 56 ÷ 8 = _____	_____ × _____ = _____
4. 84 ÷ 12 = _____	_____ × _____ = _____
5. 63 ÷ 9 = _____	_____ × _____ = _____
6. 96 ÷ 8 = _____	_____ × _____ = _____
7. 72 ÷ 9 = _____	_____ × _____ = _____
8. 64 ÷ 8 = _____	_____ × _____ = _____
9. 81 ÷ 9 = _____	_____ × _____ = _____
10. 108 ÷ 12 = _____	_____ × _____ = _____

Which Holds More?

NOTE Students compare the volumes of containers with different shapes.

Find two containers at home that you think hold about the same amount. The containers should have different shapes.

Describe your containers. You might sketch them, explain what they usually hold, or describe their shapes.

Container 1	**Container 2**

Find a way to compare the two containers to find out which holds more.

Which holds more?

Describe the method you used to compare the two containers.

Library Books

Solve each of the following problems. Show your work clearly. Be sure to answer the question posed by the story context.

NOTE Students practice solving division problems in story contexts.

SMH 38–39

1. There are 288 magazines in the library. The magazine display rack has 12 shelves. How many magazines does each shelf hold?

2. The school librarian chooses 384 books to put on display shelves. He needs to choose a bookcase for the display.

   a. If he chooses a case with 8 shelves, how many books will go on each shelf?

   b. If he chooses a case with 16 shelves, how many books will go on each shelf?

   c. If he chooses a case with 13 shelves, how many books will go on each shelf, and how many will be left over?

Multiplication Starter Problems

NOTE Students practice flexibility with solving multiplication problems.

SMH **30–32**

Solve each problem two ways, using the first steps listed below. Show your work clearly.

1. $39 \times 45 =$ _____

Start by solving $40 \times 45 =$ _____.

Start by solving $30 \times 45 =$ _____.

2. $125 \times 32 =$ _____

Start by solving $100 \times 32 =$ _____.

Start by solving $125 \times 10 =$ _____.

The Pyramids at Giza (page 1 of 2)

NOTE Students calculate and compare the volume of Egyptian pyramids, calculate the perimeter of the bases, and demonstrate the 3:1 relationship between rectangular prisms and pyramids with the same base and height.

SMH 114

The Egyptian Pharaoh Khufu built what we know today as the Great Pyramid in the ancient city of Giza circa 2550 B.C. It stood 481 feet high and each side of its square base was 756 feet long. Years later (circa 2490 B.C.), Pharaoh Menkaure started constructing another pyramid nearby. At its completion, this pyramid had a height of 215 feet and a square base of 344 by 344 feet.

1. Compare the volume of the Great Pyramid to that of Pharaoh Menkaure's and find the difference in volume between the two. Show your work in the space provided.

   The Great Pyramid: _____ cubic feet

   Pharaoh Menkaure's Pyramid: _____ cubic feet

   Difference in Volume: _____ cubic feet

The Pyramids at Giza (page 2 of 2)

2. Suppose you visit Giza and walk around the entire base of the Great Pyramid. The following day, you walk around the entire base of Pharaoh Menkaure's Pyramid. How much distance have you covered in these two walks?

3. Imagine you are designing a modern building that will be in the shape of a rectangular prism. You want the base and the height to be identical to that of the Great Pyramid. What will the volume (in cubic feet) of your building be? What if you chose to use the dimensions of Pharaoh Menkaure's pyramid?

Parrot Fire Kris Northern

"Rather than zoom into the fractal you can zoom into the edge of it and continually find the same pattern repeating itself much like the shoreline of a lake viewed from a plane." – **Kris Northern**

Investigations
IN NUMBER, DATA, AND SPACE®

Thousands of Miles, Thousands of Seats

Addition and Subtraction Problems

> **NOTE** Students solve addition and subtraction problems in which multiples of 10, 100, and 1,000 are added to and subtracted from 4-digit numbers.
>
> **SMH** 6

1. 3,267 + 10 = _____

2. 3,267 − 10 = _____

3. 3,267 + 50 = _____

4. 3,267 − 50 = _____

5. 3,267 + 100 = _____

6. 3,267 − 100 = _____

7. 3,267 + 500 = _____

8. 3,267 − 500 = _____

9. 9,702 − 10 = _____

10. 9,702 + 300 = _____

11. 9,702 − 20 = _____

12. 9,702 + 500 = _____

13. 9,702 − 200 = _____

14. 9,702 + 5,000 = _____

15. 9,702 − 2,000 = _____

16. 9,702 + 10,000 = _____

17. Choose one of the above problems, and explain how you found the answer.

Ongoing Review

18. 8,003 − 600 = _____

A. 5,003   **B.** 7,400   **C.** 7,403   **D.** 8,403

Numbers on the 10,000 Chart (page 1 of 2)

1. Label these squares on the 10,000 chart:

9,970	3,770	1,508	5,020	8,854
7,305	2,965	6,351	7,642	2,020
9,033	4,139	1,215	3,290	6,897
4,786	115	490	8,460	5,645

In Problems 2–16, find each number described below, and write the equation that shows the addition or subtraction. Label the new square on the 10,000 chart. Work with your small group on this, but each of you should complete these pages.

Example:

What number is 3 rows below 1,250? _____1,550_____
Equation: __1,250 + 300 = 1,550__

What number is:

2. 1 row below 750? _____   Equation: _____

3. 5 rows below 750? _____   Equation: _____

4. 12 rows below 750? _____   Equation: _____

5. 4 rows above 750? _____   Equation: _____

6. 40 rows below 750? _____   Equation: _____

Numbers on the 10,000 Chart (page 2 of 2)

What number is:

7. 15 rows below 5,275? _____   Equation: _____

8. 30 rows above 5,275? _____   Equation: _____

9. 25 rows above 5,275? _____   Equation: _____

10. 42 rows below 5,275? _____   Equation: _____

11. 17 rows above 5,275? _____   Equation: _____

What number is:

12. 2 rows above 10,000? _____   Equation: _____

13. 34 rows above 10,000? _____   Equation: _____

14. 11 rows above 10,000? _____   Equation: _____

15. 44 rows above 10,000? _____   Equation: _____

16. 80 rows above 10,000? _____   Equation: _____

Solve Two Ways

Solve each problem in two ways.
Record your strategy for each solution.

NOTE Students practice flexibility with solving multiplication problems.

SMH 30–32

1. 46×39

First way:	Second way:

2. 63×34

First way:	Second way:

Ongoing Review

3. This number of tiles will make a rectangle that is 6 tiles wide.

A. 36   **B.** 26   **C.** 22   **D.** 3

Adding in the Thousands

Solve each addition problem below and show your solutions.

NOTE Students practice solving addition problems. Encourage students to use one strategy and then double-check with a different strategy.

SMH **8–9**

1. $4,658 + 320 =$ _____

2. $1,956$
       $+6,504$
       $\overline{}$

3. $8,300 + 2,527 =$ _____

How Many Steps to 10,000? (page 1 of 2)

For each problem below, find out how many steps it is from the given number to 10,000 on the 10,000 chart. Use the 10,000 chart if it will help you. Show how you figured out your answer. For Problem 5, choose your own starting number.

Example:

Start at 8,500. How many steps is it to 10,000? ___1,500___

Here are two different strategies for solving the problem:

8,500 + 500 = 9,000
9,000 + 1,000 = 10,000

$$\begin{array}{r} 10,000 \\ -\ 1,000 \\ \hline 9,000 \\ -\ 500 \\ \hline 8,500 \end{array}$$

$$\begin{array}{r} 1,000 \\ +\ 500 \\ \hline 1,500 \end{array}$$

500 + 1,000 = 1,500

1. Start at 73. How many steps is it to 10,000? _____

2. Start at 3,498. How many steps is it to 10,000? _____

How Many Steps to 10,000? (page 2 of 2)

3. Start at 8,006. How many steps is it to 10,000? _____

4. Start at 450. How many steps is it to 10,000? _____

5. Start at _____. How many steps is it to 10,000? _____

Close to 1,000 Recording Sheet

Game 1   **Score**

Round 1:

____ ____ ____ + ____ ____ ____ = ____ ____ ____   ____ ____

Round 2:

____ ____ ____ + ____ ____ ____ = ____ ____ ____   ____ ____

Round 3:

____ ____ ____ + ____ ____ ____ = ____ ____ ____   ____ ____

Round 4:

____ ____ ____ + ____ ____ ____ = ____ ____ ____   ____ ____

Round 5:

____ ____ ____ + ____ ____ ____ = ____ ____ ____   ____ ____

Final Score: _____

Game 2   **Score**

Round 1:

____ ____ ____ + ____ ____ ____ = ____ ____ ____   ____ ____

Round 2:

____ ____ ____ + ____ ____ ____ = ____ ____ ____   ____ ____

Round 3:

____ ____ ____ + ____ ____ ____ = ____ ____ ____   ____ ____

Round 4:

____ ____ ____ + ____ ____ ____ = ____ ____ ____   ____ ____

Round 5:

____ ____ ____ + ____ ____ ____ = ____ ____ ____   ____ ____

Final Score: _____

Multiplication Starter Problems

NOTE Students practice flexibility with solving multiplication problems.

SMH 30–32

Solve each problem in two ways.
Record your strategy for each solution.

1. $38 \times 42 =$ _____

   Start by solving 30×40.

   Start by solving 38×10.

2. $207 \times 15 =$ _____

   Start by solving 207×10.

   Start by solving 200×15.

Ongoing Review

3. Which number is **not** a factor of 56?

   A. 6   **B.** 7   **C.** 8   **D.** 14

What Is the Missing Number?

NOTE Students find the difference between given numbers and multiples of 1,000.

SMH 6

Solve the following problems and show your solutions.

1. 4,991 + _____ = 5,000

2. 4,991 + _____ = 6,000

3. 4,991 + _____ = 8,000

4. 4,991 + _____ = 10,000

5. 1,212 + _____ = 2,000

6. 1,212 + _____ = 5,000

7. 1,212 + _____ = 9,000

8. 1,212 + _____ = 10,000

9. 3,485 + _____ = 5,000

10. 3,485 + _____ = 6,000

11. 3,485 + _____ = 8,000

12. 3,485 + _____ = 10,000

Related Problems (page 1 of 2)

Solve these sets of problems. Think about how each
problem in the set is related to the previous one.

---

1. 5,050 + 450 = _____

5,050 + 453 = _____

5,053 + 453 = _____

5,053 + 463 = _____

2. 7,000 − 30 = _____

8,000 − 30 = _____

8,010 − 30 = _____

8,010 − 38 = _____

---

3. 10,175 − 25 = _____

10,175 − 125 = _____

10,175 − 128 = _____

4. 15,560 + 1,200 = _____

15,560 + 1,250 = _____

15,560 + 1,259 = _____

---

5. 25,530 + 300 = _____

25,530 + 410 = _____

25,530 + 520 = _____

25,530 + 526 = _____

6. 9,040 − 100 = _____

9,040 − 110 = _____

9,040 − 120 = _____

9,040 − 130 = _____

Related Problems (page 2 of 2)

7. $8,474 - 500 =$ _____

$8,474 - 499 =$ _____

$8,474 - 489 =$ _____

$8,474 - 479 =$ _____

8. $134,560 + 3,000 =$ _____

$134,560 + 3,500 =$ _____

$134,565 + 3,500 =$ _____

$134,575 + 3,500 =$ _____

9. $2,000 + 1,265 =$ _____

$1,900 + 1,265 =$ _____

$1,800 + 1,265 =$ _____

$1,800 + 1,275 =$ _____

10. $90,945 - 1,000 =$ _____

$90,945 - 1,200 =$ _____

$90,945 - 1,210 =$ _____

$90,945 - 1,310 =$ _____

More How Many Steps Problems

For each problem below, find out how many steps it is from the given number to 10,000 on the 10,000 chart. Use the 10,000 chart if it will help you. Show how you figured out your answer. For Problems 4 and 5, choose your own starting number.

1. Start at 852. How many steps to 10,000? _____

2. Start at 6,105. How many steps to 10,000? _____

3. Start at 7,001. How many steps to 10,000? _____

4. Start at _____. How many steps to 10,000? _____

5. Start at _____. How many steps to 10,000? _____

Division Practice 1

Solve each division problem below. Then write the related multiplication combination.

NOTE Students review division problems that are related to the multiplication combinations they know.

SMH 14, 25–29

Division Problem	Multiplication Combination
1. $63 \div 7 =$ _____	_____ × _____ = _____
2. $72 \div 9 =$ _____	_____ × _____ = _____
3. $56 \div 8 =$ _____	_____ × _____ = _____
4. $42 \div 6 =$ _____	_____ × _____ = _____
5. $121 \div 11 =$ _____	_____ × _____ = _____
6. $84 \div 7 =$ _____	_____ × _____ = _____
7. $48 \div 8 =$ _____	_____ × _____ = _____
8. $36 \div 9 =$ _____	_____ × _____ = _____
9. $7\overline{)42}$	_____ × _____ = _____
10. $9\overline{)54}$	_____ × _____ = _____

More Related Problems

Solve these sets of problems. Think about how each problem in the set is related to the previous one.

NOTE Students solve sets of related problems. Encourage them to solve each problem mentally.

1. $4{,}580 + 250 =$ _____

$4{,}580 + 253 =$ _____

$4{,}590 + 253 =$ _____

2. $7{,}800 - 50 =$ _____

$7{,}800 - 60 =$ _____

$7{,}800 - 70 =$ _____

3. $11{,}398 + 2{,}000 =$ _____

$11{,}398 + 2{,}100 =$ _____

$11{,}398 + 2{,}150 =$ _____

4. $24{,}356 + 400 =$ _____

$24{,}356 + 410 =$ _____

$24{,}356 + 419 =$ _____

5. $14{,}532 - 3{,}000 =$ _____

$14{,}532 - 2{,}999 =$ _____

$14{,}532 - 2{,}989 =$ _____

6. $55{,}436 - 20{,}000 =$ _____

$55{,}436 - 19{,}000 =$ _____

$55{,}436 - 19{,}100 =$ _____

Sums of 1,000

Use these digits to create addition problems in which each problem has a sum of 1,000.

NOTE Students use a set of digits to create addition problems in which each problem has a sum of 1,000.

SMH 8–9

6   5   8   3   1   2   4

1. 387 + ____ ____ ____ = 1,000

2. 185 + ____ ____ ____ = 1,000

3. ____ ____ ____ + 517 = 1,000

4. 1,000 = 584 + ____ ____ ____

5. 1,000 = ____ ____ ____ + 369

6. Choose one problem above and explain how you found your answer.

Ongoing Review

7. What is the difference between 7,769 and 10,000?

    A. 3,331   **B.** 3,231   **C.** 2,231   **D.** 2,031

Thousands of Miles, Thousands of Seats

Subtraction Problems (page 1 of 2)

Solve each problem in two ways. Record your strategy for each solution.

1. $1,569 - 275 = $ _____

First way:	Second way:

2. There are 813 students in Talisha's school.
Today, 768 are present. How many are absent?

First way:	Second way:

Subtraction Problems (page 2 of 2)

3. Mitch had $10.13 in his wallet. On the way home from school he spent $5.79. How much money does he have left?

First way:	Second way:

4.

$$1,205$$
$$-\ 625$$

First way:	Second way:

Name _____

Date _____

Daily Practice

Division Practice 2

Solve each division problem below. Then write the related multiplication combination.

NOTE Students review division problems that are related to the multiplication combinations they know.

 SMH 14, 25–29

Division Problem	Multiplication Combination
1. $32 \div 4 =$ _____	_____ $\times$ _____ $=$ _____
2. $72 \div 8 =$ _____	_____ $\times$ _____ $=$ _____
3. $28 \div 7 =$ _____	_____ $\times$ _____ $=$ _____
4. $42 \div 7 =$ _____	_____ $\times$ _____ $=$ _____
5. $88 \div 11 =$ _____	_____ $\times$ _____ $=$ _____
6. $84 \div 12 =$ _____	_____ $\times$ _____ $=$ _____
7. $45 \div 5 =$ _____	_____ $\times$ _____ $=$ _____
8. $81 \div 9 =$ _____	_____ $\times$ _____ $=$ _____
9. $3\overline{)18}$	_____ $\times$ _____ $=$ _____
10. $8\overline{)96}$	_____ $\times$ _____ $=$ _____

Practicing Subtraction

Solve each subtraction problem and
show your solutions.

NOTE Students practice
solving subtraction problems
presented in different ways.

SMH 10–13

1. 734 − 566 = _____

2.   2,462
        − 1,269

3. Nora had $12.75. She spent $4.95 on baseball cards.
How much money does she have left?

4. There are 524 students at Adams School. Today,
47 are absent. How many students are at school?

Thousands of Miles, Thousands of Seats

Map of the Continental United States

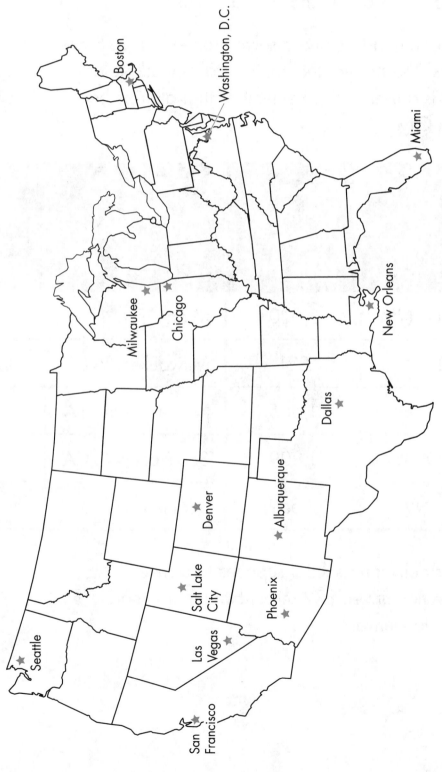

Distances (page 1 of 2)

The Descartes Trucking Company is based in New York City, New York. They guarantee delivery of anything and everything to points across the United States.

Use the mileage chart below to solve Problems 1–5. Show all your work. The map of the continental United States on page 25 is a useful tool. Remember that all trips begin in New York City.

City	Distance (in miles) from New York City	City	Distance (in miles) from New York City
Albuquerque, NM	2,020	Miami, FL	1,281
Chicago, IL	821	Milwaukee, WI	914
Dallas, TX	1,565	New Orleans, LA	1,324
Denver, CO	1,809	San Francisco, CA	2,946
Las Vegas, NV	2,559	Seattle, WA	2,894

1. Walter is delivering school supplies to Denver. So far he has driven 872 miles. How many more miles is it to Denver?

Distances (page 2 of 2)

2. Rachel is driving a trailer of new cars to Dallas. She is 480 miles from Dallas. How many miles has she driven so far?

3. On her next trip, Rachel drives a moving truck to San Francisco. She has driven 1,389 miles. How many more miles is it to San Francisco?

4. Walter is delivering a truck full of canned goods to New Orleans. On the first day he drives 489 miles, and on the second day he drives 616 miles. How many miles is he from New Orleans?

5. On their next trips, Rachel drives to Seattle and Walter drives to Milwaukee. How many more miles does Rachel drive than Walter?

Solving Division Problems

NOTE Students practice solving division problems.

SMH **38–39**

1. **a.** Write a story problem that represents 704 ÷ 22.

   b. Solve 704 ÷ 22. Show your solution clearly.

2. **a.** Write a story problem that represents $18\overline{)450}$.

   b. Solve $18\overline{)450}$.

Ongoing Review

3. Which number is a multiple of 24?

   A. 58   **B.** 76   **C.** 84   **D.** 96

Distances from New York City (page 1 of 2)

NOTE Students solve subtraction problems involving distances between cities.

 10–13

The Descartes Trucking Company is based in New York City, New York. They guarantee delivery of anything and everything to points across the United States. Use the mileage chart below to solve Problems 1–4. Show all your work. The map of the United States on page 25 is a useful tool. Remember that all trips begin in New York City.

City	Distance (in miles) from New York City	City	Distance (in miles) from New York City
Albuquerque, NM	2,020	Las Vegas, NV	2,559
Chicago, IL	821	Miami, FL	1,281

1. Charles is driving a trailer of new cars to a dealer in Chicago. He has driven 395 miles. How far is he from Chicago?

Distances from New York City (page 2 of 2)

2. Lourdes is delivering new and used furniture to Miami and is 350 miles away. How many miles has she driven?

3. Charles is driving a truck to Las Vegas. On the first day, he drives 620 miles, and on the second day, he drives 585 miles. How many more miles does he have to drive?

4. On one trip, Lourdes drove to Albuquerque. On her next trip, she drove to Las Vegas. How many more miles did she drive on the second trip?

Starter Problems (page 1 of 2)

For each of Problems 1–4, three different ways to start are shown. Solve each start, and then choose two of the starts and solve the rest of the problem. (If you start a different way, or if your class is using a different strategy, you may use that as one of your two ways.)

1. $2,168 - 455 =$

    a. $2,168 - 400 =$ **b.** $455 + 45 =$ **c.** $2,168 - 460 =$

2. $\begin{array}{r} 1,208 \\ -\ 297 \\ \hline \end{array}$

    a. $1,208 - 200 =$ **b.** $297 + 3 =$ **c.** $1,208 - 300 =$

Starter Problems (page 2 of 2)

3. 6,563
     −1,418

    a. $6{,}563 - 1{,}400 =$ **b.** $1{,}418 + 82 =$ **c.** $6{,}563 - 1{,}500 =$

4. $9{,}711 - 3{,}825 =$

    a. $9{,}711 - 3{,}000 =$ **b.** $3{,}825 + 75 =$ **c.** $9{,}711 - 4{,}000 =$

More Subtraction Problems

Solve each subtraction problem and
show your solutions.

NOTE Students practice
solving subtraction problems.

SMH 10–13

1. 1,205 − 732 = _____

2. 1,486 − 650 = _____

3. 2,550
  − 67
  ‾‾‾‾

Ongoing Review

4. Cecilia had $36.00 and she spent $19.86. How much
money did she have left?

A. $26.14   **B.** $17.16   **C.** $16.26   **D.** $16.14

Thousands of Miles, Thousands of Seats

The U.S. Algorithm (page 1 of 3)

Solve the following problems by using the U.S. algorithm. (You may want to solve the problem by using a different strategy to make sure that your final answer is correct.)

In Problems 1 and 2, the steps of the U.S. algorithm are shown. Fill in the blanks with the correct numbers.

1. 863
     −247

800	+	60	+	3
− (200	+	40	+	7)

       5
     86̸13
     −247

800	+	_____	+	_____
− (200	+	40	+	7)
_____	+	_____	+	_____

2. 325
     −164

300	+	20	+	5
− (100	+	60	+	4)

       2
     3̸125
     −164

_____	+	_____	+	5
− (100	+	60	+	4)
_____	+	_____	+	_____

The U.S. Algorithm (page 2 of 3)

For Problems 3 and 4, use the U.S. algorithm to solve each problem. Also write the correct numbers in the blanks, showing how you broke apart the original numbers.

3. 498   400   +   90   +   8
   −279   − (200   +   70   +   9)

     4 9 8   _____ + _____ + _____
    −2 7 9
                − (_____ + _____ + _____)

                _____ + _____ + _____

4. 523   500   +   20   +   3
   −292   − (200   +   90   +   2)

     5 2 3   _____ + _____ + _____
    −2 9 2
                − (_____ + _____ + _____)

                _____ + _____ + _____

The U.S. Algorithm (page 3 of 3)

For Problem 5, use the U.S. algorithm to solve the problem.
Also write the correct numbers in the blanks, showing how
you broke apart the original numbers.

5. 720   700   +   20   +   0
      −499   − (400   +   90   +   9)
      ─────   ──────────────────────

       7 2 0   _____ + _____ + _____
      −4 9 9
                  − (_____ + _____ + _____)
                    ─────────────────────────────────
                    _____ + _____ + _____

More Starter Problems (page 1 of 2)

For each of Problems 1–4, three different ways to start are shown. Solve each start, and then choose two of the starts and solve the rest of the problem. (If you start a different way, or if your class is using a different strategy, you may use that as one of your two ways.)

1. 3,402
    −1,618

   a. $3,402 − 1,000 =$ **b.** $1,618 + 82 =$ **c.** $3,404 − 1,620 =$

2. $6,847 − 2,272 =$

   a. $6,847 − 2,200 =$ **b.** $2,272 + 28 =$ **c.** $6,847 − 2,300 =$

More Starter Problems (page 2 of 2)

3. 4,103
    − 867

    a. 4,103 − 800 =   **b.** 867 + 33 =   **c.** 4,103 − 900 =

4. 11,697 − 4,225 =

    a. 11,697 − 4,000 =   **b.** 4,225 + 75 =   **c.** 11,700 − 4,225 =

Thousands of Miles, Thousands of Seats

Distances from Chicago (page 1 of 2)

The Pascal Moving Company moves people from Chicago, Illinois, to other parts of the United States. Use the mileage chart below to answer the following questions. The map of the continental United States on page 25 is a useful tool. Show all your work. Remember that all trips begin in Chicago.

City	Distance (in miles) from Chicago, IL	City	Distance (in miles) from Chicago, IL
Albuquerque, NM	1,335	Phoenix, AZ	1,800
Boston, MA	1,015	Salt Lake City, UT	1,403
Las Vegas, NV	1,761	San Francisco, CA	2,148
Miami, FL	1,377	Seattle, WA	2,072
New Orleans, LA	929	Washington, DC	715

1. Avery is driving the truck to Phoenix. He has driven 552 miles. How many miles is he from Phoenix?

Distances from Chicago (page 2 of 2)

2. Olivia is driving to San Francisco. If she is 1,674 miles from San Francisco, how far has she driven?

3. Avery is driving to Salt Lake City. On the first day, he drives 325 miles, and on the second day, he drives 459 miles. How far is he from Salt Lake City?

4. One week, Olivia drove to Boston. For her next trip, she drove to Seattle. How many more miles did she drive for the second trip?

5. Olivia drives to Las Vegas and Avery drives to Albuquerque. How many more miles does Olivia drive than Avery?

Division Practice 3

Solve each division problem below.
Then write the related multiplication
combination.

> **NOTE** Students review division problems
> that are related to the multiplication
> combinations they know.
>
> SMH **14, 25–29**

Division Problem	Multiplication Combination
1. 144 ÷ 12 = _____	_____ × _____ = _____
2. 32 ÷ 8 = _____	_____ × _____ = _____
3. 28 ÷ 4 = _____	_____ × _____ = _____
4. 56 ÷ 7 = _____	_____ × _____ = _____
5. 110 ÷ 11 = _____	_____ × _____ = _____
6. 64 ÷ 8 = _____	_____ × _____ = _____
7. 63 ÷ 9 = _____	_____ × _____ = _____
8. 27 ÷ 3 = _____	_____ × _____ = _____
9. 7)‾49‾	_____ × _____ = _____
10. 9)‾81‾	_____ × _____ = _____

Ongoing Review

11. Which number is **not** on the multiple tower for 18?

A. 54   **B.** 108   **C.** 180   **D.** 192

Subtraction Practice

Solve each subtraction problem and show your solutions.

NOTE Students have been practicing different ways to solve subtraction problems and writing their solutions using clear and concise notation.

 SMH 10–13

1. 4,835 − 2,540 = _____

2. Tavon has 773 baseball cards in his collection. Janet has 1,215 in hers. How many more cards does Tavon need to collect in order to have the same number as Janet?

3.   6,789
      − 2,199
      _____

4. 2,205 − 1,789 = _____

Daily Practice

Teams

Solve each of the following problems. Show your work clearly. Be sure to answer the question posed by the story context.

NOTE Students practice solving multiplication problems presented in story contexts.

 SMH 30–32

1. There are 38 teams and 26 students on each team. How many students play on these teams?

2. There are 56 teams in the soccer tournament. Each team has 16 players. How many soccer players are in the tournament?

3. There are 67 teams in the youth football league. Each team has 28 players. How many football players are there?

4. There are 59 teams entered in the relay race for Field Day. Each team has 32 people. How many people are entered in the relay race?

Ongoing Review

5. $18 \times 57 =$ _____

   A. 1,026   **B.** 970   **C.** 556   **D.** 513

Distance Problems (page 1 of 2)

The Pascal Moving Company moves people from Chicago, Illinois, to other parts of the United States. Use the mileage chart below to answer the following questions. The map of the United States on page 25 is a useful tool. Show all your work. Remember that all trips begin in Chicago.

NOTE Students solve subtraction problems involving distances between cities.

SMH 10–13

City	Distance (in miles) from Chicago IL	City	Distance (in miles) from Chicago IL
Miami, FL	1,377	Seattle, WA	2,072
Phoenix, AZ	1,800	San Francisco, CA	2,148

1. Tyler is driving to Miami. He has driven 888 miles. How far is he from Miami?

Distance Problems (page 2 of 2)

2. Tyler is driving to San Francisco. The first day he drives 426 miles, the second day he drives 645 miles, and the third day he drives 580 miles. How many miles is he from San Francisco?

3. Alicia is driving to Seattle. If she is 439 miles from Seattle, how many miles has she driven?

4. Alicia drives to Phoenix, and Tyler drives to Miami. How many more miles does Alicia drive than Tyler?

Close to 7,500 Recording Sheet

Game 1   **Score**

Round 1:

____ ____ ____ ____ + ____ ____ ____ ____ = ____ ____   ____

Round 2:

____ ____ ____ ____ + ____ ____ ____ ____ = ____ ____   ____

Round 3:

____ ____ ____ ____ + ____ ____ ____ ____ = ____ ____   ____

Round 4:

____ ____ ____ ____ + ____ ____ ____ ____ = ____ ____   ____

Round 5:

____ ____ ____ ____ + ____ ____ ____ ____ = ____ ____   ____

Final Score: _____

Game 2   **Score**

Round 1:

____ ____ ____ ____ + ____ ____ ____ ____ = ____ ____   ____

Round 2:

____ ____ ____ ____ + ____ ____ ____ ____ = ____ ____   ____

Round 3:

____ ____ ____ ____ + ____ ____ ____ ____ = ____ ____   ____

Round 4:

____ ____ ____ ____ + ____ ____ ____ ____ = ____ ____   ____

Round 5:

____ ____ ____ ____ + ____ ____ ____ ____ = ____ ____   ____

Final Score: _____

Library Books

Solve each of the following problems. Show your work clearly. Be sure to answer the question posed by the story context.

NOTE Students practice solving division problems in story contexts.

 SMH 38–39

1. There are 512 biographies in the school library. If each shelf holds 26 books, how many shelves are completely filled? How many books are left?

2. There are 462 magazines in the library. Each shelf holds 14 magazines. How many shelves hold magazines?

3. There were 378 books donated to the local school libraries. There are 9 schools in town now. If the books are distributed evenly, how many books does each school library receive?

4. There were 374 magazines donated to an elementary school. There are 22 classrooms in the school now. If the magazines are distributed equally, how many magazines will each classroom receive?

Ongoing Review

5. Which is equal to 18×50?

    A. 36×100 **B.** 9×25 **C.** 9×100 **D.** 180×500

More or Less Than 7,500?

Students are playing *Close to 7,500* and made these numbers with their digit cards. What is the sum of their cards? What is their score? Show all your work.

> **NOTE** Students practice addition in the context of a game called "Close to 7,500." The score is the difference between the sum of the numbers and 7,500.
>
> **SMH** 8–9

1. $6,821 + 894 =$ Score _____

2. $4,207 + 2,845 =$ Score _____

3. $2,415 + 5,097 =$ Score _____

4. $3,780 + 3,749 =$ Score _____

Stadium and Arena Capacities

The following tables show the seating capacities of a number of fictitious stadiums and arenas. You will need these data to complete pages 52–55 and pages 59–62.

Football and Baseball Stadiums		
Grand Canyon Stadium	Tempe, AZ	73,521
Garden State Stadium	East Rutherford, NJ	78,741
Gopherdome	Minneapolis, MN	64,035 (football) 55,883 (baseball) 40,000 (basketball, concerts)
Empire Stadium	New York, NY	57,545
Sunshine Stadium	Los Angeles, CA	56,000
Cajundome	New Orleans, LA	69,703 (football) 20,000 (concerts) 55,675 (basketball) 63,525 (baseball)
Patriot Park	Boston, MA	33,993

Arenas		
Copper State Arena	Phoenix, AZ	19,023
Jersey Arena	East Rutherford, NJ	20,049
Big Apple Arena	New York, NY	19,763
Minutemen Center	Boston, MA	18,624 (basketball) 19,600 (concerts)
Badger Arena	Milwaukee, WI	18,600 (basketball) 20,000 (concerts)
Golden State Arena	Los Angeles, CA	20,000

Filling Up and Emptying (page 1 of 4)

Use the data about stadium and arena capacities on page 51 to solve Problems 1–13 on pages 52–55. Remember to show the equations you use to solve the problems. You should be able to do most of these problems mentally.

In Problems 1–3, people are going to a sold-out basketball game at the Golden State Arena.

1. The game starts at 7:30 P.M. At 7:00 P.M., 9,000 people are in their seats. How many people are not at the game yet?

2. **a.** At 7:45 P.M., 5,000 more people have come and are in their seats. How many people are there now?

   b. How many people are not at the game yet?

3. At 8:00 P.M., all but 1,500 people are at the game. How many people are now at the game?

Filling Up and Emptying (page 2 of 4)

In Problems 4–6, people are going to a football game at the Gopherdome.

4. The game is sold out. At the end of the third quarter, the game is not close, so 10,000 people go home. How many people are still in the stadium?

5. With 10 minutes left in the game, 20,000 more people go home. How many people are still in the stadium?

6. At the end of the game, another 25,000 people leave. The others stay to wait for the traffic to clear. How many people are still in the stadium?

Filling Up and Emptying (page 3 of 4)

In Problems 7–10, people are going to a football game at the Cajundome.

7. The game starts at 7:00 P.M. There were 2,500 tickets that were not sold. How many people will be attending the game?

8. At 6:00 P.M., 10,000 people were in the Cajundome. How many people were not there yet? (Remember that not all seats were sold.)

9. **a.** At 7:00 P.M., 37,800 more people had come. How many people are there now? (Remember that not all seats were sold.)

   b. How many people have not shown up yet?

10. Eventually, everyone who had a ticket had come to the game. At halftime, 25,000 people were not in their seats. How many people were still seated?

Filling Up and Emptying (page 4 of 4)

For Problems 11–13, pick a stadium or arena: _____

11. People are attending a sold-out concert there. Thirty minutes before it starts, 15,000 people are there. How many people have not arrived yet?

12. By the time the concert starts, all but 1,300 people have shown up. How many people are at the concert?

13. Everyone finally showed up, but 3,200 people leave before the end. How many people are still there?

Addition and Subtraction Practice

NOTE Students practice solving addition and subtraction problems.

SMH 8–9, 10–13

Solve the following problems. Show your work clearly.

1. 34,500 + 964 = _____

2. 34,500 − 1,255 = _____

3. 15,465 + 3,223 = _____

Ongoing Review

4. A concert hall holds 12,655 people. 10,443 tickets were sold. How many tickets are left?

A. 2,212   **B.** 2,213   **C.** 2,222   **D.** 3,222

Subtracting Numbers in the Thousands

NOTE Students practice solving subtraction problems with larger numbers.

SMH 10–13

Solve each problem below. Use clear and concise notation to show how you solved each problem.

1. 7,249 − 4,832 = _____

2. 16,207 − 8,112 = _____

3.   21,462
        − 8,993
       _____

Rock On! (page 1 of 4)

Use the data about stadium and arena capacities on page 51 to the solve Problems 1–13 on pages 59–62. Record how you solved the problems, using clear and concise notation.

The Composites, the hottest rock band in the United States, have decided to go on tour. Their good friends, the Square Roots, will be the opening band.

1. The Composites are deciding whether they should play Jersey Arena or Big Apple Arena. How many more seats are there in Jersey Arena than in Big Apple Arena?

2. The band decides to play both Jersey Arena and Big Apple Arena. They sell all the tickets for both concerts. How many tickets are sold?

3. The band wants to know how many more tickets they would be able to sell if they played at Garden State Stadium instead of Grand Canyon Stadium.

4. The Composites and the Square Roots play at sold-out concerts at the Gopherdome, Sunshine Stadium, and the Minutemen Center. How many tickets did they sell for these three concerts?

Rock On! (page 2 of 4)

In Problems 5–8, the Composites and the Square Roots decide to play a benefit concert at Empire Stadium that starts at 3:00 P.M.

5. At 2:00 P.M., 40,895 people are already in the stadium. How many more people can the stadium hold?

6. **a.** At 3:00 P.M., as the Square Roots start to play, 12,472 more people have arrived. How many people are in the stadium now?

   b. How many more people can the stadium hold?

7. By 4:00 P.M., every seat has been taken. As the Composites are setting up, 49,083 people are in their seats, and the others have gone to the concession stands. How many people are at the concession stands?

8. 38,012 people buy souvenirs at the concert. How many people do not buy souvenirs?

Rock On! (page 3 of 4)

9. The Composites and Square Roots play at sold-out
   concerts at Patriot Park and Copper State Arena.
   How many tickets were sold?

10. The bands sell all but 500 tickets for an 8:00 P.M.
    concert at Badger Arena. At 7:30 P.M., 18,777
    people have arrived. How many people are not
    at the arena yet?

11. **a.** The bands play at a sold-out concert at Minutemen
    Center. At 7:00 P.M., 11,456 people are in the arena.
    At 7:30 P.M., 6,845 more people have arrived. How
    many people have not shown up?

    b. Everyone has finally arrived at the concert at
    Minutemen Center. After the Square Roots play,
    4,219 people leave their seats to buy refreshments
    or souvenirs. How many people are still in
    their seats?

Rock On! (page 4 of 4)

In Problems 12 and 13, the Composites and the Square Roots play at a sold-out concert at Grand Canyon Stadium that begins at 5:00 P.M.

12. a. At 4:00 P.M., 62,106 people are in the stadium. How many more people are expected to show up?

b. At 4:30 P.M., 10,500 more people have arrived. How many people are at the concert now?

c. How many people have not yet arrived?

13. As the Composites start to play, everyone has arrived. 64,086 people are in their seats, and the others are at the concession stands. How many people are at the concession stands?

Make Your Own Story

For the past several days, you have been working with
the data about stadium and arena capacities on page 51.
This is your chance to make up your own story about
people coming and going to some sort of event at one of
these stadiums or arenas. You should not spend more than
15 minutes writing your story.

1. Decide on an event (concert, game, and so on). _____

2. Decide on a stadium or arena for the event. _____

3. Write 3 to 5 problems about your event.

4. On a separate sheet of paper, solve your
own problems.

Marching Band

NOTE Students practice solving multiplication and division problems in story problem contexts.

SMH 30–32, 38–39

Solve each of the following problems. Show your work clearly. Be sure to answer the question posed by the context.

There are 216 students in the school marching band.

1. The director wants the band to march in rows with 12 students in each row. How many rows will there be?

2. For an inside assembly, the band needs to fit on the stage with 24 students in each row. How many rows will there be now?

3. The marching band is raising money for new uniforms. If each student in the band sells 12 raffle tickets, how many tickets will they sell?

4. New T-shirts cost $24 each. How much will it cost to buy a new T-shirt for each student in the band?

Ongoing Review

5. $189 \div 27 =$ _____

   A. 9   **B.** 7   **C.** 6 R17   **D.** 5 R14

Practicing Addition and Subtraction

NOTE Students practice solving addition and subtraction problems.

SMH 8–9, 10–13

Solve each of the following problems.
Show your work clearly.

1. $9,124 + 4,279 =$ _____

2.
$$\begin{array}{r} 8,569 \\ -2,895 \\ \hline \end{array}$$

3. $9,201 - 7,225 =$ _____

4. $4,550 + 8,872 =$ _____

Mystery Tower

The top part of Felix's multiple tower is shown.
Answer these questions about his tower.

> **NOTE** On this page, students practice solving multiplication and division problems.
>
> **SMH** 20

1. By what number did Felix count?
How do you know?

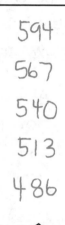

594
567
540
513
486

2. How many numbers are in Felix's tower so far?
How do you know?

3. Write a multiplication equation that represents how many numbers are in Felix's multiple tower.

_____ × _____ = _____

4. What is the 10th multiple in Felix's tower? _____

5. Imagine that Felix adds more multiples to his tower.

a. What would be the 20th multiple in his tower? _____
How do you know?

b. What would be the 25th multiple in his tower? _____
How do you know?

Concert Time

Solve these problems and record your solutions, using clear and concise notation.

NOTE Students practice solving addition and subtraction problems.

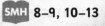 **SMH** 8–9, 10–13

The Composites are playing at a sold-out concert at the Gopherdome, which holds 40,000 people. The concert starts at 8:00 P.M. Answer the questions below and show your work.

1. At 7:00 P.M., 28,175 people are at the concert. How many people have not arrived yet?

2. **a.** By 7:30 P.M., 9,590 more people have arrived. How many people are at the concert now?

   b. How many people have not arrived yet?

3. By 8:00 P.M., all but 1,642 people are at the concert. How many people are at the concert now?

Go Climb a Mountain

NOTE Students solve real-world problems involving the math content of this unit.

SMH 10–13

Daily Practice

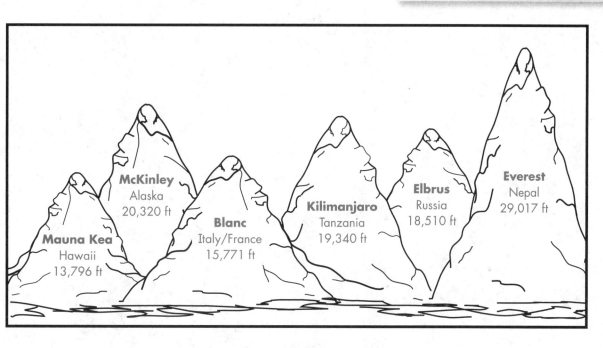

Everest
Nepal
29,017 ft

Elbrus
Russia
18,510 ft

McKinley
Alaska
20,320 ft

Kilimanjaro
Tanzania
19,340 ft

Blanc
Italy/France
15,771 ft

Mauna Kea
Hawaii
13,796 ft

The diagram shows the height, in feet, of some of the world's highest mountains. Answer the following questions. Solve as many of these problems mentally as you can.

1. Mt. Everest was first measured in 1856. The height was recorded as 29,000 feet. The measurement given above for Mt. Everest was made in 2005. How much greater is it?

2. How much taller is Mt. McKinley than Mt. Kilimanjaro?

3. Mauna Kea is the tallest mountain in the world when measured from its base on the ocean floor. 16,000 feet of the mountain is under water. What is the total height of Mauna Kea, measuring from the base in the ocean to the summit above the ocean?

"Rather than zoom into the fractal you can zoom into the edge of it and continually find the same pattern repeating itself much like the shoreline of a lake viewed from a plane." – **Kris Northern**

Investigations
IN NUMBER, DATA, AND SPACE®

What's That Portion?

What Do You Already Know? (page 1 of 2)

Answer the questions below.

1. In one group, 2 out of 5 students are wearing glasses.
   a. What fraction is that?

   b. What fraction is not wearing glasses?

2. **a.** Tyler cut his small pizza into sixths. He ate the
      whole pizza. How many pieces did he eat?

   b. Alicia cut her pizza into eighths. She ate half
      of the pizza. How many pieces did she eat?

3. In one class, $\frac{1}{6}$ of the students raked leaves while the
   rest picked up trash on the playground. What fraction
   of the students picked up trash?

4. A spelling pretest had 14 words.
   a. Cecilia spelled 100% of the words correctly.
      How many words did she spell correctly?

   b. Yumiko spelled only 7 of the 14 words correctly.
      What percent of the words did she spell correctly?

What Do You Already Know? (page 2 of 2)

Answer the questions below.

5. a. Avery wins $\frac{1}{3}$ of these marbles.
Draw a circle around them.

b. Hana wins $\frac{2}{3}$ of the marbles.
How many marbles does she win?

6. When 8 children go on a picnic, $\frac{6}{8}$ of them wear jeans.
a. How many wear jeans?

b. What fraction does not wear jeans?

7. True or False? Circle T or F. Explain how you know.
Use a picture if it helps.

a. $\frac{2}{3} > \frac{2}{6}$ T   F

b. $\frac{1}{4} < \frac{2}{8}$ T   F

c. $1 = \frac{1}{3} + \frac{1}{2} + \frac{1}{6}$ T   F

How Far to 10,000?

Imagine that you have a long number line that goes from 0 to 10,000. Find these distances on the number line.

> **NOTE** Students use addition and subtraction to solve problems about the difference between some number and 10,000.
>
> SMH 8–9, 11

0   10,000

1. How far is it on the number line from 4,590 to 10,000?

2. How far is it on the number line from 7,002 to 10,000?

3. How far is it on the number line from 648 to 10,000?

4. How far is it on the number line from 5,151 to 10,000?

5. How far is it on the number line from 93 to 10,000?

Everyday Uses of Fractions, Decimals, and Percents

List in the spaces below the everyday uses you find for fractions, decimals, and percents. Cut out your examples from used magazines and newspapers, and attach them to this sheet.

NOTE Students look for everyday uses of fractions, decimals, and percents, which will be added to a list the class started today.

 40

Everyday Uses of Fractions	Everyday Uses of Decimals

Everyday Uses of Percents

Name the Shaded Portion

Below each grid, name the percent and some fractions
to describe the portion that is shaded.

Grid 1

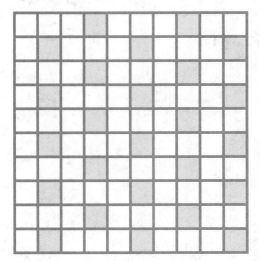

Percent: _____

Fractions: _____

Grid 2

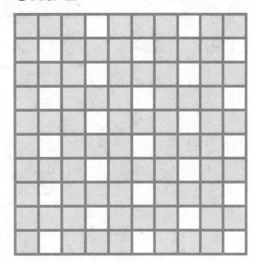

Percent: _____

Fractions: _____

Grid 3

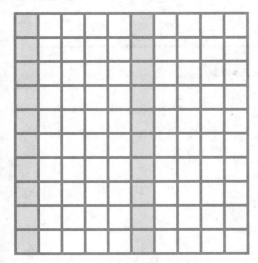

Percent: _____

Fractions: _____

Grid 4

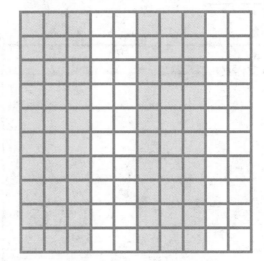

Percent: _____

Fractions: _____

Solve Two Ways, Addition

Solve each problem in two ways. Use clear and concise notation in your solutions.

NOTE Students work on flexibility in choosing solution strategies for solving addition problems.

SMH 8–9

1. $6,725 + 2,373 =$ _____

First way:	Second way:

2. $\begin{array}{r} \$143.85 \\ + \ 66.37 \\ \hline \end{array}$

First way:	Second way:

What Fractions Do You See?

> **NOTE** Students identify fractional parts of a group and write equivalent fractions that represent each part. They can choose their family, a group of friends, or some other group.
>
> **SMH** 42, 44

Write statements about a small group of people, such as family members or friends, just as we did in class. Draw the group and the characteristic you are describing, and record the fraction that represents each statement. Write equivalent fractions that you know.

Example: <u>2</u> out of <u>6</u> people <u>have black hair</u>. Fraction: $\frac{2}{6} = \frac{1}{3}$

This is the group I am describing:

_____ out of _____ people _____. Fraction: _____

_____ out of _____ people _____. Fraction: _____

_____ out of _____ people _____. Fraction: _____

_____ out of _____ people _____. Fraction: _____

_____ out of _____ people _____. Fraction: _____

10 × 10 Grids

1.

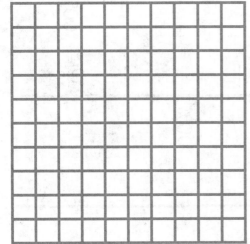

Fraction: $\dfrac{}{100}$

Percent: _____%

2.

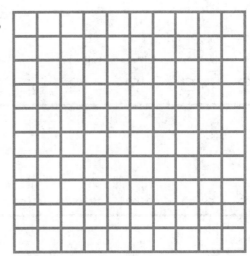

Fraction: $\dfrac{}{100}$

Percent: _____%

3.

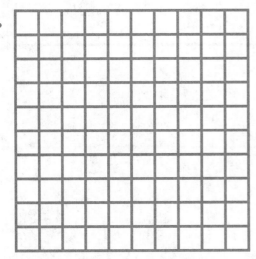

Fraction: $\dfrac{}{100}$

Percent: _____%

4.

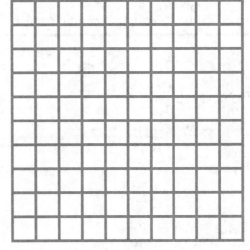

Fraction: $\dfrac{}{100}$

Percent: _____%

Fraction and Percent Equivalents

$$\frac{1}{10} = \underline{\quad}$$ $$\frac{2}{10} = \underline{\quad}$$ $$\frac{3}{10} = \underline{\quad}$$ $$\frac{4}{10} = \underline{\quad}$$ $$\frac{5}{10} = \underline{\quad}$$ $$\frac{6}{10} = \underline{\quad}$$ $$\frac{7}{10} = \underline{\quad}$$ $$\frac{8}{10} = \underline{\quad}$$ $$\frac{9}{10} = \underline{\quad}$$ $$\frac{10}{10} = 100\%$$

$$\frac{1}{8} = \underline{\quad}$$ $$\frac{2}{8} = \underline{\quad}$$ $$\frac{3}{8} = \underline{\quad}$$ $$\frac{4}{8} = \underline{\quad}$$ $$\frac{5}{8} = \underline{\quad}$$ $$\frac{6}{8} = \underline{\quad}$$ $$\frac{7}{8} = \underline{\quad}$$ $$\frac{8}{8} = 100\%$$

$$\frac{1}{6} = \underline{\quad}$$ $$\frac{2}{6} = \underline{\quad}$$ $$\frac{3}{6} = \underline{\quad}$$ $$\frac{4}{6} = \underline{\quad}$$ $$\frac{5}{6} = \underline{\quad}$$ $$\frac{6}{6} = 100\%$$

$$\frac{1}{5} = \underline{\quad}$$ $$\frac{2}{5} = \underline{\quad}$$ $$\frac{3}{5} = \underline{\quad}$$ $$\frac{4}{5} = \underline{\quad}$$ $$\frac{5}{5} = 100\%$$

$$\frac{1}{4} = \underline{\quad}$$ $$\frac{2}{4} = \underline{\quad}$$ $$\frac{3}{4} = \underline{\quad}$$ $$\frac{4}{4} = 100\%$$

$$\frac{1}{3} = \underline{\quad}$$ $$\frac{2}{3} = \underline{\quad}$$ $$\frac{3}{3} = 100\%$$

$$\frac{1}{2} = \underline{\quad}$$ $$\frac{2}{2} = 100\%$$

Fractions of 100

Write the fraction for the shaded part of each grid. Then write the percent.

NOTE Students identify the fractional part of a square that is shaded. They represent it with a fraction and a percent.

SMH 47–49

1.
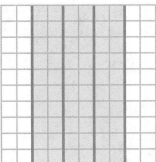

Fraction: _____

Percent: _____

2.
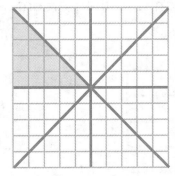

Fraction: _____

Percent: _____

3.
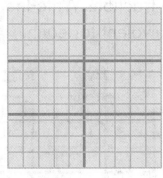

Fraction: _____

Percent: _____

Ongoing Review

4. Beth has 60 toy cars and trucks. 75% of them are blue. How many are blue?

A. 75 **B.** 45 **C.** 30 **D.** 15

What's That Portion?

Seeing Fractions and Percents on Grids

NOTE Students use 10 × 10 grids to find fraction and percent equivalents.

SMH 47–49

For each grid below, choose a fraction and color in the portion of the grid that represents the fraction. Write the fraction and the percent equivalent for each.

1.

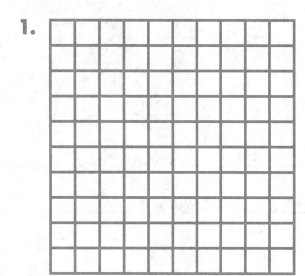

_____ = _____ = _____%
              100

2.

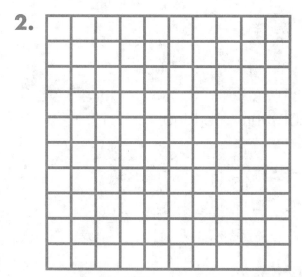

_____ = _____ = _____%
              100

Match the Fraction and Percent

NOTE Students match fractions and percents to the shaded part of a square.

SMH 47–49

Write the letter of each grid to the fractions and percent that describe the shaded part of the grid.

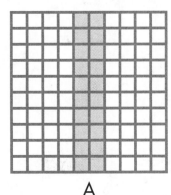

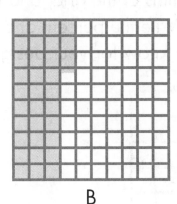

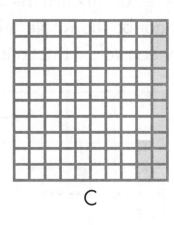

A   B   C

1. $\frac{2}{10}$ _____

2. $\frac{1}{3}$ _____

3. $33\frac{1}{3}\%$ _____

4. $\frac{1}{8}$ _____

5. $12\frac{1}{2}\%$ _____

6. $\frac{1}{5}$ _____

7. $\frac{20}{100}$ _____

8. 20% _____

Ongoing Review

9. Sharon and Fred bought a blueberry pie. Sharon ate $\frac{4}{6}$ of the pie. Fred ate $\frac{1}{3}$ of the pie. How much of the pie did they eat altogether?

A. $\frac{1}{3}$ of the pie

C. $\frac{5}{9}$ of the pie

B. $\frac{1}{2}$ of the pie

D. $\frac{3}{3}$ of the pie

Designs on Grids

On each grid below, draw and color in a design. Then determine the fractional part and percent of the grid you have colored. Your design cannot be $\frac{1}{2}$, $\frac{1}{4}$, $\frac{3}{4}$, or any number of tenths of the grid, and it cannot be the whole grid. Write the percent and any equivalent fractions you know for your design.

NOTE Students use 10 × 10 grids to find fraction and percent equivalents.

 47–49

1.

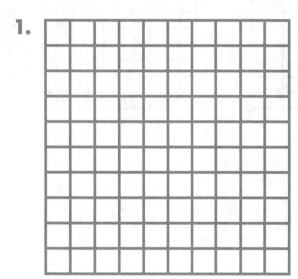

_____ = _____ = _____%
               100

2.

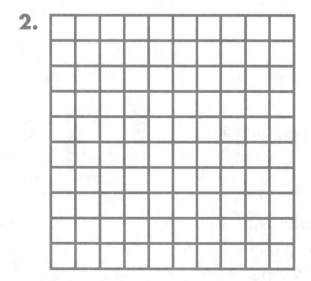

_____ = _____ = _____%
               100

School Days (page 1 of 2)

Solve these problems.

1. **a.** In a class of 30 students, 50% went to the library. How many students went to the library?

   b. At the same time, 10 of the students helped with the canned food drive.

   What fractional part of the class is that? _____

   What percentage is that? _____

   c. The rest of the students stayed in the classroom to finish their homework.

   What fraction of students stayed in the classroom? _____

   What percent is that? _____

   d. The next day, $66\frac{2}{3}\%$ of the students brought cans of food for the food drive. How many students brought in cans of food?

2. **a.** A spelling pretest had 20 words. Janet spelled 10 of them correctly. What percent of the words did she spell correctly?

   b. Benito spelled 75% of the words correctly. How many words did he spell correctly?

School Days (page 2 of 2)

Solve these problems.

3. There are 50 students in the fifth grade at Clark School. One day, 20% of them were absent. How many fifth graders were in school that day? Show how you figured out your answer.

4. **a.** There are 64 fifth graders at Parks School. $\frac{3}{8}$ of them bring their own lunch to school. How many of them bring their own lunch? Show how you figured out your answer.

   b. What percentage of the fifth graders bring their lunch to school?

Solve Two Ways, Subtraction

NOTE Students work on flexibility in choosing solution strategies for solving subtraction problems.

 SMH 10–13

Solve each problem in two ways. Use clear and concise notation in your solutions.

1. 8,593
   −2,748
   _____

First way:	Second way:

2. 12,500 − 3,670 = _____

First way:	Second way:

Finding Fraction Equivalents

> **NOTE** Students find equivalent fractions and percents. Students will know some of these equivalents easily and may draw pictures to figure out others.
>
> **SMH** 47–49

List as many fractions as you can that are equal to the percent listed.

For example: $50\% = \dfrac{1}{2}, \dfrac{2}{4}, \dfrac{3}{6}, \dfrac{4}{8}, \dfrac{5}{10}, \dfrac{50}{100}, \dfrac{100}{200}$

1. $33\frac{1}{3}\% =$ _____

2. $25\% =$ _____

3. $40\% =$ _____

4. $75\% =$ _____

5. $80\% =$ _____

The Percent Trail

Markers show where these fractions are located along the trail.

> **NOTE** Students put fractions and percents in order along a "trail." This trail provides a visual image of fraction-percent equivalents, like those they are working on in class.
>
> **SMH** 46–51

$\frac{1}{2}$　　$\frac{1}{3}$　　$\frac{2}{3}$　　$\frac{1}{4}$　　$\frac{3}{4}$　　$\frac{2}{5}$　　$\frac{3}{5}$　　$\frac{4}{5}$　　$\frac{1}{6}$　　$\frac{1}{8}$　　$\frac{5}{8}$

1. Finish the markers by writing the fractions on them.

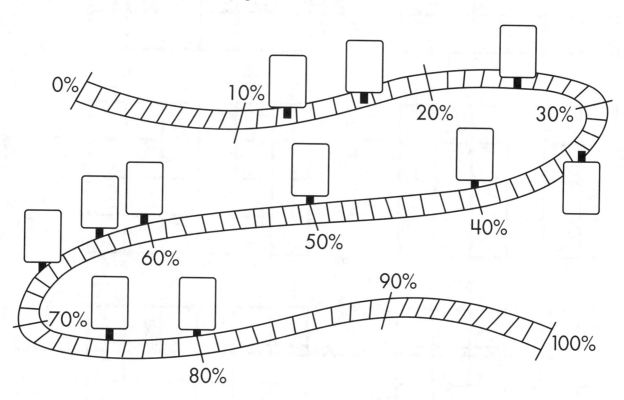

Ongoing Review

2. Cross out the equation that is **not** true.

A. $50\% = \frac{1}{2}$　　　　**C.** $75\% = \frac{3}{4}$

B. $30\% = \frac{1}{3}$　　　　**D.** $\frac{1}{10} = 10\%$

Shading 4 × 6 Rectangles

Shade $\frac{7}{8}$ of the first rectangle. Shade $\frac{5}{6}$ of the second rectangle.

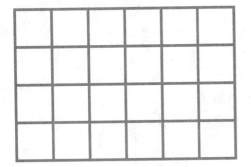

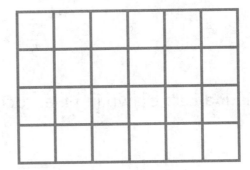

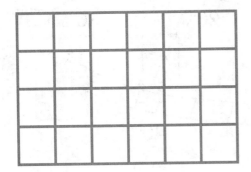

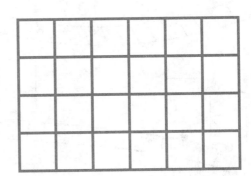

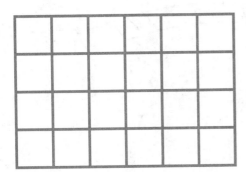

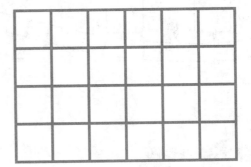

Which Is Greater? (page 1 of 2)

Solve the problems below and explain or show how you
determined the answer.

1. Which is greater? $\frac{7}{10}$ or $\frac{3}{5}$

2. Which is greater? $\frac{7}{8}$ or $\frac{9}{10}$

3. Which is greater? $\frac{4}{3}$ or $\frac{3}{4}$

4. Which is greater? $\frac{3}{8}$ or $\frac{1}{3}$

Which Is Greater? (page 2 of 2)

Solve the problems below and explain or show how you determined the answer.

5. Which is greater? $\frac{3}{5}$ or $\frac{1}{2}$

6. Janet and Martin each got a pizza for lunch, and each pizza is the same size. Janet cut hers into 3 pieces and ate 1 piece. Martin cut his pizza into 5 pieces and ate 2 pieces. Who ate more pizza?

7. Charles and Rachel each got a pizza, and each pizza is the same size. Charles cut his pizza into 8 pieces. For lunch he ate $\frac{1}{2}$ of the pizza, and for a snack he ate 1 more piece. Rachel cut her pizza into 10 pieces. For lunch she ate 4 pieces, and for a snack she ate 2 more pieces. Who ate more pizza?

8. Mercedes and Nora each got some frozen yogurt for a treat. Mercedes ate $\frac{3}{8}$ of her yogurt, and Nora ate $\frac{3}{4}$ of her yogurt. They agree that they ate the same amount of yogurt. Explain how that could be true. Use a picture or diagram to show your ideas.

Related Problems

Solve the related problems in each set below. As you work on these problems, think about how solving the first problem in each set may help you solve the others.

NOTE Students practice solving addition and subtraction problems in related sets. Ask students what they notice about the place value of the digits in the sums or differences in each set.

1. $3{,}040 + 260 =$ _____

$3{,}040 + 263 =$ _____

$3{,}140 + 263 =$ _____

2. $6{,}600 - 20 =$ _____

$7{,}600 - 20 =$ _____

$7{,}610 - 20 =$ _____

3. $9{,}532 - 3{,}000 =$ _____

$9{,}532 - 2{,}999 =$ _____

$9{,}532 - 2{,}989 =$ _____

4. $12{,}420 + 600 \quad =$ _____

$12{,}420 + 1{,}600 =$ _____

$12{,}420 + 1{,}637 =$ _____

5. $34{,}740 + 200 =$ _____

$34{,}740 + 300 =$ _____

$34{,}740 + 330 =$ _____

$34{,}740 + 333 =$ _____

6. $15{,}030 - 100 =$ _____

$15{,}030 - 120 =$ _____

$15{,}030 - 140 =$ _____

$15{,}030 - 145 =$ _____

Comparing $\frac{2}{3}$ and $\frac{3}{4}$

NOTE Students write what they know about $\frac{2}{3}$ and $\frac{3}{4}$ and explain which one is greater.

SMH 50–51

1. Write at least three statements showing what you know about the fraction $\frac{2}{3}$. Think about equivalent fractions, percents, how this fraction is related to 1 or $\frac{1}{2}$, or other things you know.

2. Write at least three statements showing what you know about the fraction $\frac{3}{4}$.

3. Find two different ways to show how you know whether $\frac{3}{4}$ is greater than $\frac{2}{3}$.

Goal!

NOTE Students use $\frac{1}{2}$ and 1 as reference points for fractions and percents.

SMH 50–51

1. Draw lines to put each ball in the correct goal.

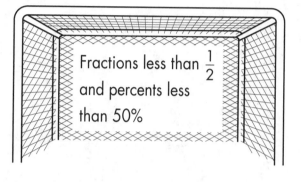

Fractions less than $\frac{1}{2}$ and percents less than 50%

Fractions between $\frac{1}{2}$ and 1 and percents between 50% and 100%

2. Is 70% greater than or less than $\frac{1}{2}$? How do you know?

Ongoing Review

3. Circle the equation that is **not** true.

A. $75\% = \frac{3}{4}$ **C.** $30\% = \frac{1}{3}$

B. $50\% = \frac{3}{6}$ **D.** $100\% = \frac{12}{12}$

Comparing $\frac{7}{8}$ and $\frac{5}{6}$

Find three ways to show that $\frac{7}{8}$ is greater than $\frac{5}{6}$.
Use pictures, numbers, and/or words.

NOTE Students compare two
fractions and explain how they
know which one is greater.

SMH 50–51

1.

2.

3.

Fraction and Percent Problems (page 1 of 2)

Solve the following problems.

1. Renaldo, Mitch, and Hana make their own pizzas.
   All three pizzas are the same size.

   a. Renaldo cut his pizza into 3 equal pieces and ate
   2 pieces. What fraction of the pizza did he eat? _____

   b. Mitch cut his pizza into 8 equal pieces and ate 5
   pieces. What fraction of the pizza did he eat? _____

   c. Hana cut her pizza into 6 equal pieces and ate
   3 pieces. What fraction of pizza did she eat? _____

   d. Who ate the most pizza? Who ate the least?
   Show how you found your answers.

2. Each runner in a relay race runs one leg, or $\frac{1}{8}$ kilometer.
   How many runners will it take to cover the $\frac{3}{4}$ kilometer?
   Explain your solution.

3. Zachary and Nora are talking about how many hits
   they got at a baseball game. Zachary hit the ball
   3 times out of 10 times at bat. Nora hit the ball 4 times
   out of 12 times at bat. Who is a better hitter in this
   game? Explain how you know.

Name _____ Date _____

Fraction and Percent Problems (page 2 of 2)

Solve the following problems.

4. Georgia and Shandra made juice smoothies and poured them equally into 2 glasses that are the same size. Georgia drank 75% of her smoothie. Shandra drank $\frac{5}{6}$ of hers. Who drank more of her smoothie? Explain how you know.

5. a. A class has 32 students. One half of them are in the lunchroom, finishing their lunch. How many students are still in the lunchroom? _____

b. At the same time, $\frac{1}{4}$ of the students are playing basketball. How many students are playing basketball? _____

c. At the same time, $12\frac{1}{2}\%$ of the students are helping in the Snack Shack. How many students are helping in the Snack Shack? _____

d. The rest of the students in the class are working on a project in the classroom. What fraction of the class is in the classroom? Explain or show how you know.

Addition Problems

Solve each problem below. Use clear and concise notation to show how you solved each problem.

NOTE Students practice solving multidigit addition problems.

SMH 8–9

1.   5,531
 +2,487

2. 4,485 + 6,223 = _____

3. 13,416 + 772 = _____

4.   31,379
 +48,013

In Between Problems

Hana and Martin are working together to play a perfect game of *In Between* in which they place all of the cards. They have each played one card. Write Hana's and Martin's fractions in the blank cards in the game to show how they can all fit.

NOTE Students have been comparing fractions by playing "In Between." In this homework, they try to place all the cards in a round of this game.

SMH **50–51, G10**

Hana's cards:

| $\frac{3}{4}$ | $\frac{2}{5}$ | $\frac{5}{6}$ | $\frac{9}{10}$ | $\frac{7}{10}$ |

Martin's cards:

| $\frac{1}{3}$ | $\frac{3}{10}$ | $\frac{1}{4}$ | $\frac{4}{5}$ | $\frac{1}{2}$ |

Game:

| 10% | $\frac{1}{8}$ | | | | | 50% | $\frac{5}{8}$ | | | | | 90% |

Ordering Fractions (page 1 of 2)

NOTE Students practice comparing and ordering fractions.

SMH 50–51

1. Write the above fractions in order.
Some are done for you.

Ordering Fractions (page 2 of 2)

2. Write the above fractions in order.
Some are done for you.

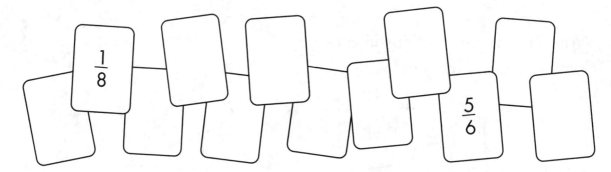

True or False?

Solve the following problems.

Decide whether these statements are true or false.
Circle TRUE or FALSE. Explain your reasoning.

Remember: > means greater than: 3 > 2
                    < means less than: 2 < 3

1. $\frac{2}{3}$ of 60 > $\frac{1}{3}$ of 120   TRUE   FALSE

2. $\frac{1}{4}$ of 32 = $\frac{1}{2}$ of 16   TRUE   FALSE

3. 75% of 100 < 75% of 120   TRUE   FALSE

Subtraction Problems

Solve each problem below. Use clear and concise notation to show how you solved each problem.

NOTE Students practice solving multidigit subtraction problems.

SMH 10–13

1.   7,348
     −6,552

2. 36,814 − 23,653 = _____

3. 8,376 + _____ = 45,791

4.   10,000
     − 3,671

More *In Between* Problems

Janet and Deon are working together to play a perfect game of *In Between* in which they place all of the cards. They have each played one card. Write Janet's and Deon's fractions in the blank cards in the game to show how they can all fit.

NOTE Students have been comparing fractions by playing "In Between". In this homework, they try to place all the cards in a round of this game.

SMH 50–51, G10

Janet's cards:

| $\frac{3}{8}$ | $\frac{5}{6}$ | $\frac{2}{3}$ | $\frac{7}{10}$ | $\frac{3}{10}$ |

Deon's cards:

| $\frac{7}{8}$ | $\frac{1}{3}$ | $\frac{4}{5}$ | $\frac{1}{4}$ | $\frac{1}{5}$ |

Game:

| 10% | $\frac{1}{6}$ | | | | | 50% | $\frac{3}{5}$ | | | | | 90% |

Clock Fractions

1. 	**2.** 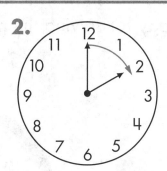	**3.** 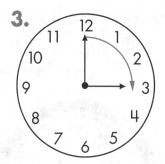
4. 	**5.** 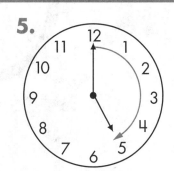	**6.** 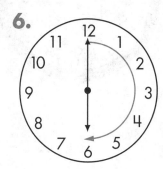
7. 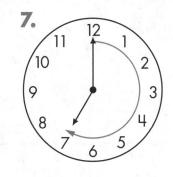	**8.** 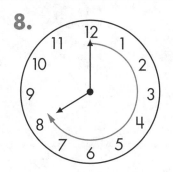	**9.** 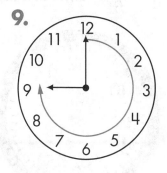
10. 	**11.** 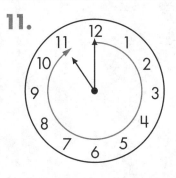	**12.** 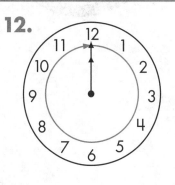

Clock Fractions Addition Problems (page 1 of 2)

For each fraction addition problem, show your work on the
clock face. Record your strategy for solving the problem.

1. $\frac{1}{4} + \frac{1}{2} =$ _____

2. $\frac{1}{4} + \frac{1}{3} =$ _____

3. $\frac{3}{4} + \frac{1}{3} =$ _____

Clock Fractions Addition Problems (page 2 of 2)

Make up your own fraction addition equations
for Problems 4 and 5.

4. _____ + _____ = _____

5. _____ + _____ = _____

True or False?

Solve the following problems.

NOTE Students find fractional parts and percents of a quantity.

SMH 40–41

Decide whether these statements are true or false.
Circle TRUE or FALSE. Explain your reasoning.

Remember: > means greater than: 3 > 2
            < means less than: 2 < 3

1. $\frac{2}{5}$ of 50 = $\frac{1}{5}$ of 100   TRUE   FALSE

2. $\frac{1}{4}$ of 200 > $\frac{1}{2}$ of 100   TRUE   FALSE

3. $12\frac{1}{2}$% of 800 < 25% of 400   TRUE   FALSE

Comparing Fractions

Choose two pairs of fractions from the following list. Use pictures, numbers, and/or words to find two ways to show which fraction is greater and to explain how you know.

> **NOTE** Students compare fractions to determine which one is greater and explain how they know.
>
> **SMH** 50–51

$\frac{1}{3}$ and $\frac{1}{4}$ $\frac{1}{2}$ and $\frac{3}{5}$ $\frac{5}{8}$ and $\frac{7}{10}$ $\frac{3}{2}$ and $\frac{4}{3}$

$\frac{9}{5}$ and $\frac{7}{4}$ $\frac{2}{3}$ and $\frac{5}{6}$ $\frac{1}{8}$ and $\frac{2}{10}$ $\frac{3}{4}$ and $\frac{4}{5}$

Pair 1: _____ and _____

1.

2.

Pair 2: _____ and _____

1.

2.

Concert Tickets

Solve each of the following problems. Show your
work clearly. Be sure to answer the question
posed by the story.

> **NOTE** Students practice
> solving subtraction problems
> in story contexts.
>
> **SMH** 10–13

1. **a.** The Composites are playing a concert at the
   Sunshine Stadium. At 10:00 A.M., 56,000 tickets
   went on sale. After 20 minutes of ticket sales,
   18,493 tickets remained. How many were sold
   in the first 20 minutes?

   b. After 45 minutes, only 3,728 tickets were left. Of
   the 56,000 original tickets, how many were sold
   after 45 minutes?

2. **a.** The Square Roots are playing a concert at the Palm
   Dome. At noon, 64,500 concert tickets went on
   sale. After an hour, 27,483 tickets were sold. How
   many remain?

   b. After two hours, 43,893 tickets were sold. Of the
   original 64,500 original tickets, how many remain?

Roll Around the Clock Problems

Nora and Alexander are playing *Roll Around the Clock*. For each round, find the sum of their rolls and circle who wins the point. If it is a tie, write "tie" next to the round.

NOTE Using the distance around a clock as a model, students practice adding fractions with related denominators.

SMH 52–53, G12–G13

Nora: Alexander:

Round 1:

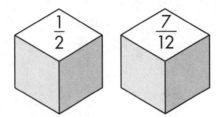
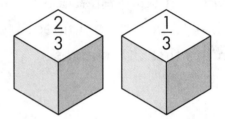

sum: _____   sum: _____

Round 2:

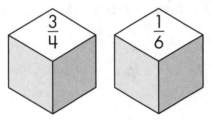
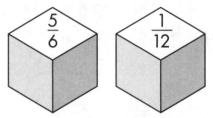

sum: _____   sum: _____

Round 3:

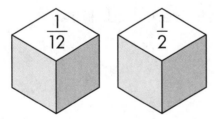
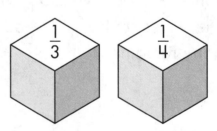

sum: _____   sum: _____

Round 4:

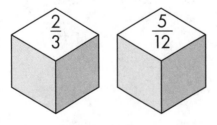
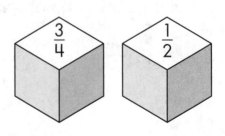

sum: _____   sum: _____

Using Rectangles to Add Fractions

Choose either the 4×6 or 5×12
rectangles to show how to solve $\frac{1}{3} + \frac{5}{12} =$ _____.

4×6 Rectangles

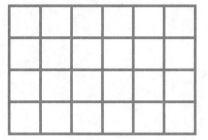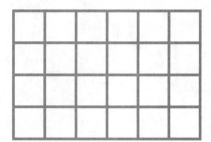

5×12 Rectangles

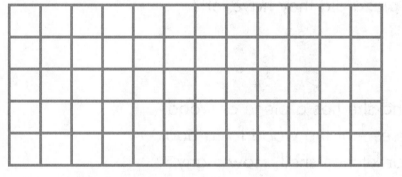

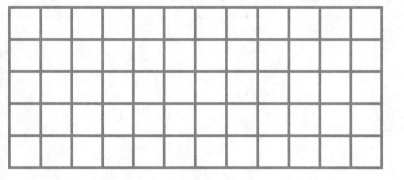

Adding and Subtracting Fractions

Solve each problem below. Explain how you found the answer.

1. $\frac{1}{4} + \frac{2}{3} = $ _____

2. $\frac{1}{6} + \frac{1}{2} + \frac{1}{4} = $ _____

3. A pizza is cut into 12 equal pieces. Alexander eats $\frac{1}{3}$ of the pizza, Rachel eats $\frac{1}{4}$ of the pizza, and Charles eats $\frac{1}{12}$. What fraction of pizza did they have left?

4. Georgia is a carpenter, and she has a piece of wood that is 10 feet long. She uses $\frac{1}{2}$ of the wood for a book shelf and $\frac{1}{4}$ of the wood for kitchen shelf. How many feet of wood are left? What fraction of the whole piece is that?

5. $\frac{3}{12} + \frac{1}{2} + \frac{2}{3} = $ _____

Roll Around the Clock Equations

Choose a round from the *Roll Around the Clock* game in which you rolled the fraction cubes only **twice** during your turn, and record it as an addition equation.

For example: $1\frac{1}{12} = \frac{1}{3} + \frac{3}{4}$ $\frac{5}{12} + \frac{7}{12} = 1$

1. The fractions I rolled were: _____.

   Addition equation: _____

2. The fractions I rolled were: _____.

   Addition equation: _____

3. The fractions I rolled were: _____.

   Addition equation: _____

Choose a round from the *Roll Around the Clock* game in which you rolled the fraction cubes **more than two times**, and record it as an addition equation.

For example: $1 = \frac{2}{3} + \frac{1}{4} + \frac{1}{12}$ $\frac{7}{12} + \frac{1}{3} + \frac{1}{6} = 1\frac{1}{12}$

4. The fractions I rolled were: _____.

   Addition equation: _____

5. The fractions I rolled were: _____.

   Addition equation: _____

Which Is Closer to 1? Part 1

Find the two totals. Then circle the one that is closer to 1.
Show how you figured out the sums.

NOTE Students add
fractions and compare
the sums.

 SMH 50–53

1. $\frac{1}{2} + \frac{7}{12} =$ _____ $\frac{1}{6} + \frac{2}{3} =$ _____

2. $\frac{1}{4} + \frac{1}{3} =$ _____ $\frac{1}{6} + \frac{1}{2} =$ _____

Ongoing Review

3. Samantha won 8 out of the 10 tennis matches she
played. What percentage of the games did she win?

A. 8%   **B.** 80%   **C.** $\frac{8}{10}$%   **D.** 10%

Practice Adding Fractions

Solve the problems below, explaining your work.

> **NOTE** Students use different models (including the clock or rectangles) and their understanding of equivalent fractions to add fractions.
>
> **SMH** **52–53**

Alexander, Rachel, and Olivia had a pizza party. There was a pepperoni, a vegetarian, and a cheese pizza. Each pizza was the same size.

1. Alexander ate $\frac{1}{6}$ of the pepperoni pizza and $\frac{5}{12}$ of the cheese pizza. How much of a pizza did he eat?

2. Rachel ate $\frac{1}{8}$ of the vegetarian pizza and $\frac{1}{4}$ of the cheese pizza. How much of a pizza did she eat?

3. Olivia ate $\frac{1}{6}$ of the pepperoni pizza, $\frac{1}{3}$ of the vegetarian pizza, and $\frac{1}{6}$ of the cheese pizza. How much of a pizza did she eat?

4. $\frac{1}{5} + \frac{3}{10} = $ _____

5. $\frac{2}{3} + \frac{5}{6} = $ _____

Fraction Tracks (page 1 of 2)

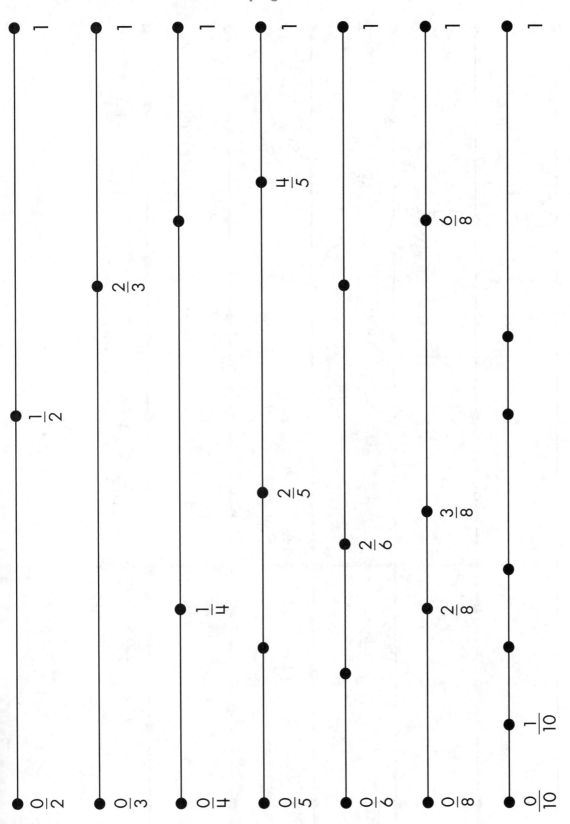

Fraction Tracks (page 2 of 2)

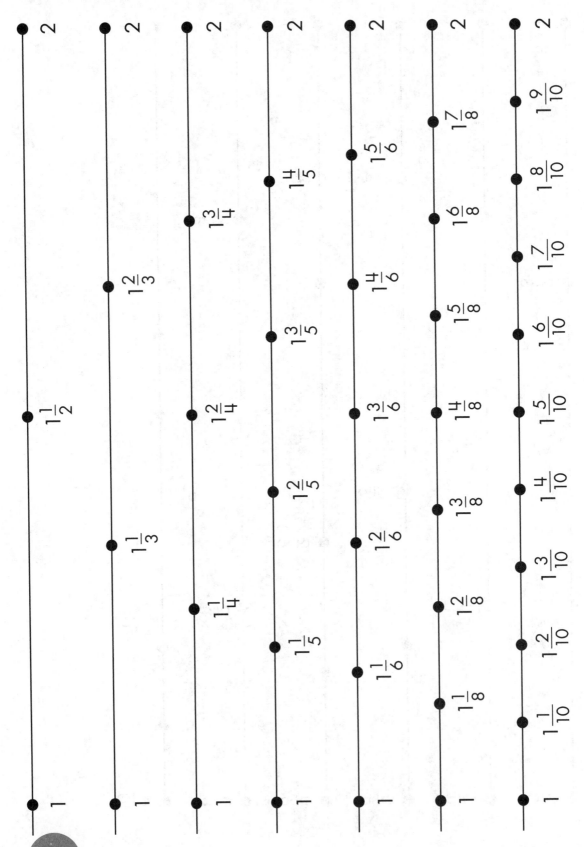

Reading Challenge

Solve each of the following problems. Show your work clearly. Be sure to answer the question posed by the story.

NOTE Students practice solving subtraction problems in story contexts.

SMH 10–13

1. A city library held a reading challenge to see how many books the students could read in June, July, and August. They hoped that the students would read a total of 20,000 books. By the end of June, the students had read 6,837 books. How many more books did they need to read to reach 20,000 books?

2. By the end of July, the students had read 14,288 books. How many more books did they need to read in August in order to read 20,000 altogether?

3. In all, the students read 22,681 books this summer. Next year the library will increase the reading challenge goal to 25,000 books. How many more books will that be, compared with the total they read this summer?

4. Last summer, students in the city read 17,589 books. If they read 22,681 this summer, how many more books did they read?

Which Is Closer to 1? Part 2

NOTE Students add fractions and compare the sums.

SMH **50–53**

Find the two totals. Then circle the one that is closer to 1. Show how you figured out the sums.

1. $\dfrac{5}{10} + \dfrac{2}{5} =$ _____ $\dfrac{4}{12} + \dfrac{2}{4} =$ _____

2. $\dfrac{3}{4} + \dfrac{1}{4} =$ _____ $\dfrac{2}{8} + \dfrac{2}{4} =$ _____

Ongoing Review

3. Felix loves to play checkers. He won 150 out of the last 200 games he played. What percentage of the games did he win? Circle the answer. Show how you figured it out.

   A. 150%   **B.** 100%   **C.** 75%   **D.** 50%

More *Roll Around the Clock* Problems

Renaldo and Hana are playing *Roll Around the Clock*. For each round, find the sum of their rolls and circle who wins the point. If it's a tie, write "tie" next to the round.

NOTE Using the distance around a clock as a model, students practice adding fractions with related denominators.

SMH 52–53, G12–G13

Renaldo:

Hana:

Round 1: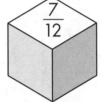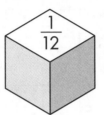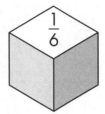

sum: _____

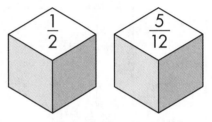

sum: _____

Round 2: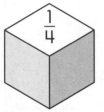

sum: _____

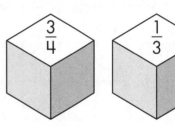

sum: _____

Round 3: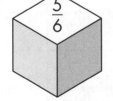

sum: _____

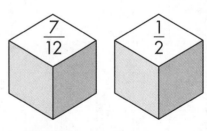

sum: _____

Round 4: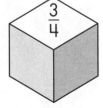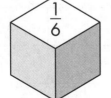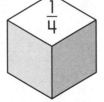

sum: _____

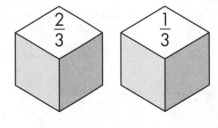

sum: _____

Tallest Mountains

This is a table of some of the world's tallest mountains. Use this table to answer the questions below. Show your work clearly.

NOTE Students practice solving addition and subtraction problems in story contexts.

SMH **8–9, 10–13**

Mountain	Continent	Height (in feet)
Mount Everest	Asia	29,035
Aconcagua	South America	22,831
Mount McKinley	North America	20,320
Mount Kilimanjaro	Africa	19,563
Mount Elbrus	Europe	18,481
Vinson Massif	Antarctica	16,066
Mount Kosciuszko	Australia (mainland)	7,310

1. How much taller is Mount Everest than Aconcagua?

2. How much taller is Mount McKinley than Mount Kosciuszko?

3. How much taller is Mount Kilimanjaro than Vinson Massif?

4. Which mountain is 1,839 feet taller than Mount Elbrus?

Equivalents

List at least 5 equivalent fractions
for each fraction below.

NOTE Students find
equivalent fractions.

SMH 44

1. $\frac{1}{2} =$

2. $\frac{1}{3} =$

3. $\frac{3}{4} =$

4. $\frac{2}{5} =$

Fraction Track Equations

Record moves that involve **more than one track** from the rounds of the *Fraction Track* game you are playing. Write your moves as addition problems.

For example: $\boxed{\dfrac{7}{8}}$ $\dfrac{7}{8} = \dfrac{1}{2} + \dfrac{1}{4} + \dfrac{1}{8}$ $\boxed{\dfrac{3}{4}}$ $\dfrac{1}{2} + \dfrac{1}{4} = \dfrac{3}{4}$

1. The fraction on my card was _____.

   Addition equation: _____

2. The fraction on my card was _____.

   Addition equation: _____

3. The fraction on my card was _____.

   Addition equation: _____

Record moves that involve moves on **two tracks** from the rounds of the *Fraction Track* game you are playing. Write your moves as addition and subtraction problems.

For example: $\boxed{\dfrac{5}{6}}$ $\dfrac{5}{6} = \dfrac{1}{2} + \dfrac{1}{3}$ $\dfrac{5}{6} - \dfrac{1}{3} = \dfrac{1}{2}$

4. The fraction on my card was _____.

   Addition equation: _____

   Subtraction equation: _____

5. The fraction on my card was _____.

   Addition equation: _____

   Subtraction equation: _____

Fraction Problems (page 1 of 3) ✏️ WRITING

Solve these problems. Show or explain how
you solved them.

1. Shandra and Tyler made two loaves of bread. On
   Monday, they ate $\frac{1}{2}$ of one loaf. On Tuesday, they
   ate $\frac{1}{3}$ of one loaf. How much bread was left?

2. $\frac{3}{8} + \frac{1}{4} + \frac{4}{4} =$ _____

3. $2 - \frac{2}{3} =$ _____

Fraction Problems (page 2 of 3)

Solve these problems. Show or explain how
you solved them.

4. There are 6 brownies on a plate. Margaret ate
   $1\frac{1}{2}$ brownies. Charles ate $2\frac{1}{4}$ brownies. Tyler
   ate $1\frac{3}{4}$ brownies. How many brownies are left
   on the plate?

5. $\frac{3}{4} + \frac{9}{6} =$ _____

6. $\frac{4}{4} - \frac{1}{3} =$ _____

Fraction Problems (page 3 of 3) WRITING

Solve these problems. Show or explain how
you solved them.

7. Is this equation true or false? $\frac{7}{8} + \frac{7}{8} = 1\frac{3}{4}$
Explain how you know.

8. Is this equation true or false? $\frac{4}{4} - \frac{2}{2} = \frac{3}{3}$
Explain how you know.

9. Cecilia is wrapping presents for her sister's birthday.
She has 10 feet of ribbon. She uses $2\frac{1}{2}$ feet to wrap
one present, $3\frac{1}{3}$ feet to wrap another present, and
$1\frac{3}{4}$ feet to wrap the third present. If she needs 2 feet
for the last present, does she have enough ribbon left?

Less Than, Greater Than, or Equal To? Part 1

Choose one of these symbols to fill in the blank to show whether the two expressions are equal or whether one is greater than the other. Explain your thinking.

> **NOTE** Students decide whether two expressions that involve addition and subtraction of fractions and mixed numbers are equal or whether one is greater than the other. Students may solve for the sum or difference of each expression, or they may be able to reason about the relationships of the fractions without actually solving. For example, in Problem 3, because $\frac{12}{8} = \frac{9}{6}$ and less is subtracted from $\frac{12}{8}$ than from $\frac{9}{6}$, the first expression must be greater than the second.
>
> **SMH** 45, 50–53

$$= \text{equal} \qquad\qquad < \text{less than} \qquad\qquad > \text{greater than}$$
$$4 + 3 = 3 + 4 \qquad\qquad 5 + 7 < 7 + 7 \qquad\qquad 6 + 6 > 5 + 5$$

1. $\frac{1}{4} + \frac{3}{4}$ _____ $\frac{3}{2} - \frac{1}{2}$

2. $\frac{10}{12} + 1\frac{1}{2}$ _____ $\frac{3}{4} + 1\frac{1}{4}$

3. $\frac{12}{8} - \frac{1}{6}$ _____ $\frac{9}{6} - \frac{1}{2}$

Missing Digits

Fill in the missing digits in each problem.
Show how you found the missing digits.

NOTE Students practice solving
addition and subtraction problems.

SMH 8–9, 10–13

1.
```
    1  2, 0  0  0
  −  ___, 9 ___ 4
  ──────────────
       5, 0  5  6
```

2.
```
       3  3 ___
       5 ___ 7
  + ___  4  8
  ──────────────
    1,  3  0  0
```

Can you find four digits to complete these problems?
Is it possible or impossible? Explain your thinking.

3. 9,724 + _____ = 20,000

4. 12,000 + _____ = 2,487

Moves on the *Fraction Track*

Imagine that you are playing the *Fraction Track* game with the board that goes from 0 to 2. All your markers are on 0. Find different combinations of ways you can move on 2 tracks, 3 tracks, or 4 tracks.

> **NOTE** Students have been playing a game in which they find different sums that equal a given fraction.
>
> **SMH** 52–53

For example, if you draw $\frac{7}{8}$, you can move:

On two tracks: $\frac{1}{2} + \frac{3}{8}$

On three tracks: $\frac{1}{2} + \frac{1}{4} + \frac{1}{8}$

On four tracks: $\frac{1}{3} + \frac{1}{6} + \frac{1}{4} + \frac{1}{8}$

Find some different ways you could move if you got these fraction cards.

1. Your fraction card is $\frac{10}{10}$. What are some ways you could move?

   On two tracks:

   On three tracks:

   On four tracks:

2. Your fraction card is $\frac{12}{8}$. What are some ways you could move?

   On two tracks:

   On three tracks:

   On four tracks:

Less Than, Greater Than, or Equal To? Part 2

NOTE Students decide whether two expressions that involve addition and subtraction of fractions and mixed numbers are equal or whether one is greater than the other. Students may solve for the sum or difference of each expression, or they may be able to reason about the relationships of the fractions without actually solving.

SMH 45, 50–53

Choose one of these symbols to put in the blank to show whether the two expressions are equal or whether one is greater than the other. Explain your thinking.

$= $ equal

$4 + 3 = 3 + 4$

$< $ less than

$5 + 7 < 7 + 7$

$> $ greater than

$6 + 6 > 5 + 5$

1. $\frac{3}{6} + \frac{4}{8} + 2$ _____ $1\frac{1}{2} + \frac{5}{10} + 1\frac{1}{4}$

2. $3\frac{3}{4} - \frac{7}{8}$ _____ $3\frac{1}{4} - \frac{6}{8}$

3. $\frac{2}{3} + 1\frac{1}{2} + \frac{6}{10}$ _____ $\frac{15}{10} + \frac{3}{5} + \frac{4}{6}$

More Moves on the Fraction Track

NOTE Students have been playing a game in which they find different sums that equal a given fraction.

SMH 52–53

Suppose that you are playing the *Fraction Track* game with the board that goes from 0 to 2. All your markers are on 0. Find different combinations of ways you can move on 2 tracks, 3 tracks, or 4 tracks.

For example, if you draw $\frac{7}{8}$, you can move:

On two tracks: $\frac{1}{2} + \frac{3}{8}$

On three tracks: $\frac{1}{2} + \frac{1}{4} + \frac{1}{8}$

On four tracks: $\frac{1}{3} + \frac{1}{6} + \frac{1}{4} + \frac{1}{8}$

Find some different ways you could move if you got these fraction cards.

1. Your fraction card is $\frac{9}{6}$. What are some ways you could move?

   On two tracks:

   On three tracks:

   On four tracks:

2. Your fraction card is $\frac{12}{10}$. What are some ways you could move?

   On two tracks:

   On three tracks:

   On four tracks:

Going the Distance (page 1 of 2)

A scout troop is going on a hiking trip to a nearby state park.

NOTE Students solve real-world problems involving the math content of this unit.

SMH 52–53

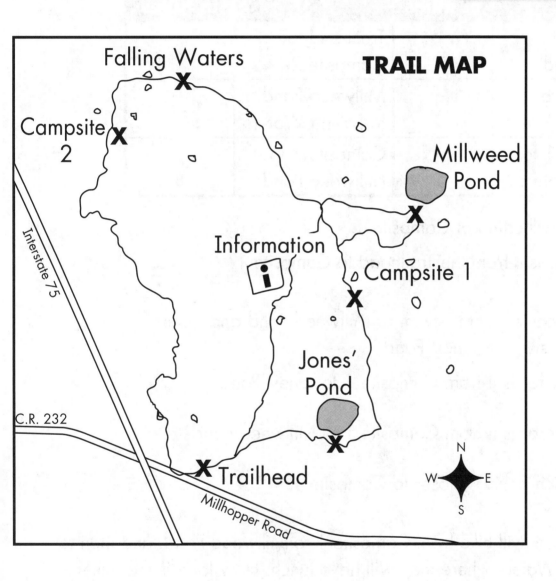

TRAIL MAP

Falling Waters

Campsite 2

Campsite 1

Millweed Pond

Information

Jones' Pond

Interstate 75

C.R. 232

Trailhead

Millhopper Road

N
W E
S

Going the Distance (page 2 of 2)

The table shows the distances along different parts of the trail.

Landmarks	Distance in miles	Landmarks	Distance in miles
Trailhead to Jones' Pond	$\frac{3}{5}$	Trailhead to Campsite 2	2
Trailhead to Campsite 1	$1\frac{1}{2}$	Millweed Pond to Falling Waters	$1\frac{1}{4}$
Campsite 1 to Falling Waters	$1\frac{1}{2}$	Campsite 1 to Millweed Pond	$\frac{7}{8}$

The scouts will camp at Campsite 1.

1. How far is it from the Trailhead to Campsite 1?

2. Some scouts want to swim at Millweed Pond and others want to swim at Jones' Pond.

    a. How far is it from Campsite 1 to Jones' Pond?

    b. How far is it from Campsite 1 to Millweed Pond?

    c. Which pond is closer to Campsite 1?

3. The scouts will hike from Campsite 1 to Millweed Pond, and then to Falling Waters where they will have lunch. How long is that hike?

4. Some scouts decide to hike back from Falling Waters to Campsite 1 along the shorter route. How much shorter will their hike be than if they go back by way of Millweed Pond?

Parrot Fire Kris Northern

"Rather than zoom into the fractal you can zoom into the edge of it and continually find the same pattern repeating itself much like the shoreline of a lake viewed from a plane." – **Kris Northern**

Investigations
IN NUMBER, DATA, AND SPACE®

Measuring Polygons

Investigation 3

Triangles: Two the Same, One Different (page 1 of 2)

In your set of Shape Cards, find two triangles that have some attribute in common. Write the numbers of these triangles and answer the questions below.

1. Triangles # _____ and _____

What is the same about these two? _____

_____

Draw two other triangles that fit with these two.

Draw a triangle that is different. Explain how it is different.

2. Triangles # _____ and _____

What is the same about these two? _____

_____

Draw two other triangles that fit with these two.

Draw a triangle that is different. Explain how it is different.

Measuring Polygons

Triangles: Two the Same, One Different (page 2 of 2)

In your set of Shape Cards, find two triangles that have some attribute in common. Write the numbers of these triangles and answer the questions below.

3. Triangles # _____ and _____

What is the same about these two? _____

_____

Draw two other triangles that fit with these two.

Draw a triangle that is different. Explain how it is different.

4. Triangles # _____ and _____

What is the same about these two? _____

_____

Draw two other triangles that fit with these two.

Draw a triangle that is different. Explain how it is different.

Which Triangle Doesn't Belong?

In each group of triangles, circle the one that does not belong. Explain how you know that it does not belong.

1.

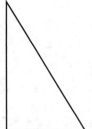 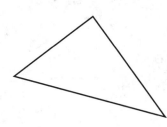 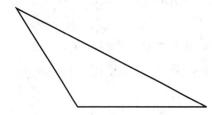

2.

 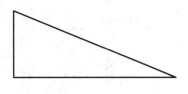 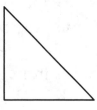

Ongoing Review

3. Which statement is true about this triangle?

  A. It has one 90° angle.

  B. All of its angles are less than 90°.

  C. It has one angle greater than 90°.

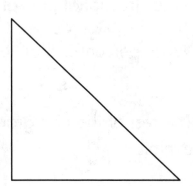

NOTE Students solve problems about fractions and percents of a group.

SMH 40–41

Field Trip Fractions and Percents

Solve the following problems. Explain how you determined your answers.

Last week 40 fifth graders went on a field trip to the science museum.

1. 25% of the students went to see the space exhibit. How many students is that? _____

2. 20 of the fifth graders went to see the technology exhibit.

What fractional part of the group is that? _____

What percent is that? _____

3. 8 of the fifth graders went to see a live animal presentation.

What fractional part of the group is that? _____

What percent is that? _____

4. The rest of the fifth graders went to the dinosaur exhibit.

What fractional part of the group is that? _____

What percent is that? _____

Quadrilaterals: Two the Same, One Different (page 1 of 2)

In your set of Shape Cards, find two quadrilaterals that have some attribute in common. Write the numbers of these quadrilaterals and answer the questions below.

1. Quadrilaterals # _____ and _____

What is the same about these two? _____

_____

Draw two other quadrilaterals that fit with these two.

Draw a quadrilateral that is different.
Explain how it is different.

2. Quadrilaterals # _____ and _____

What is the same about these two? _____

_____

Draw two other quadrilaterals that fit with these two.

Draw a quadrilateral that is different.
Explain how it is different.

Quadrilaterals: Two the Same, One Different (page 2 of 2)

In your set of Shape Cards, find two quadrilaterals that have some attribute in common. Write the numbers of these quadrilaterals and answer the questions below.

3. Quadrilaterals # _____ and _____

What is the same about these two? _____

_____

Draw two other quadrilaterals that fit with these two.

Draw a quadrilateral that is different.
Explain how it is different.

4. Quadrilaterals # _____ and _____

What is the same about these two? _____

_____

Draw two other quadrilaterals that fit with these two.

Draw a quadrilateral that is different.
Explain how it is different.

Which Quadrilateral Doesn't Belong?

In each group of quadrilaterals, circle the one that does not belong. Explain how you know that it does not belong.

NOTE Students find the quadrilateral in each group that has an attribute not shared by the other quadrilaterals in the group.

SMH 96–98

1.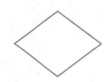

2.

Ongoing Review

3. Which statement is true about this quadrilateral?

    A. It has one set of parallel sides.

    B. It has two sets of parallel sides.

    C. It has no parallel sides.

Some Figures Have Many Names (page 1 of 3)

1. Draw a square.

Is what you drew a rhombus? Explain why or why not.

Is what you drew a rectangle? Explain why or why not.

Some Figures Have Many Names (page 2 of 3)

2. Draw a rectangle.

Is what you drew a square? Explain why or why not.

Is what you drew a parallelogram?
Explain why or why not.

Some Figures Have Many Names (page 3 of 3)

3. Draw a parallelogram, a rectangle, a rhombus, and a square.

4. Write *All*, *Some*, or *No* to complete these statements:

   a. _____ rectangles are parallelograms.

   b. _____ rectangles are squares.

   c. _____ parallelograms are rectangles.

   d. _____ squares are rectangles.

   e. _____ rhombuses are squares.

5. Choose one of the sentences in Problem 4 and explain your response. Include drawings to show what you mean.

Equivalents

List at least 5 equivalent fractions for each item.

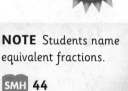

NOTE Students name equivalent fractions.

SMH 44

1. $\frac{1}{2} =$ _____

2. $\frac{2}{3} =$ _____

3. $75\% =$ _____

4. $60\% =$ _____

Squares and Rectangles

NOTE Students consider ways in which two types of quadrilaterals, squares and rectangles, are related to each other.

SMH 96–98

1. Write as many statements as you can about this square.

2. Write as many statements as you can about this rectangle.

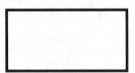

3. Explain why some statements are on both of your lists.

4. Explain why some statements are on only one of your lists.

Measuring Polygons

Which Are Regular Polygons?

Below are scale drawings of shapes made with Power
Polygons™. Tell whether each shape is a regular polygon.
Explain in writing how you know.

1. Is this a regular polygon? _____
How do you know?

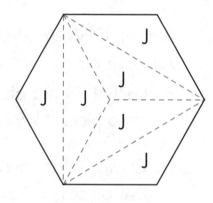

2. Is this a regular polygon? _____
How do you know?

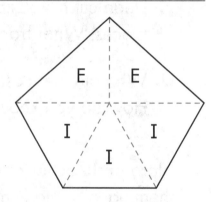

3. Is this a regular polygon? _____
How do you know?

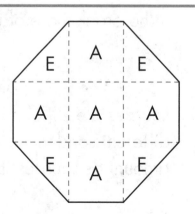

Fraction and Percent Problems

> **NOTE** Students solve problems about fractions and percents of a group.
>
> **SMH** 40–41

Solve the following problems. Explain how you determined your answers.

1. Rachel, Olivia, and Deon make their own pizzas. All three pizzas are the same size.

   a. Rachel cut her pizza into four equal pieces and ate three pieces. What fraction of the pizza did she eat?

   b. Olivia cut her pizza into eight equal pieces and ate five pieces. What fraction of the pizza did she eat?

   c. Deon cut his pizza into six equal pieces and ate five pieces. What fraction of pizza did he eat?

   d. Who ate the most pizza? Who ate the least? How do you know?

2. Nora and Zachary made juice smoothies and poured them equally into 2 glasses that are the same size. Nora drank $\frac{2}{3}$ of her smoothie. Zachary drank 75% of his. Who drank more of their smoothie? How do you know?

3. Lourdes ate 25% of a sandwich. Mitch ate 50% of a different sandwich. Mitch claims that he ate the same amount as Lourdes. Explain how this is possible.

Measuring Polygons

Parallel or Not?

Parallel lines never meet. Parallel segments or sides are parts of parallel lines.

> **NOTE** Students distinguish between different types of quadrilaterals, focusing on the attribute of parallel sides.
>
> **SMH** 97

1. Circle the shapes with exactly 1 pair of parallel sides.

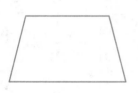   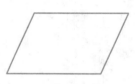

2. Circle the shapes with 2 pairs of parallel sides.

 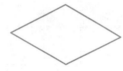 

3. Draw a shape that has
- 4 sides in all
- 2 right angles
- 1 pair of parallel sides

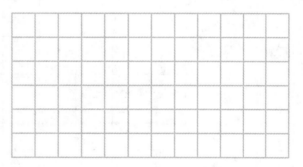

4. Explain the difference between a parallelogram and a rectangle.

_____

_____

_____

_____

Measuring Polygons

Angles in the Power Polygons (page 1 of 3)

Label each angle with its measure. Explain how
you figured out the measure of each angle.

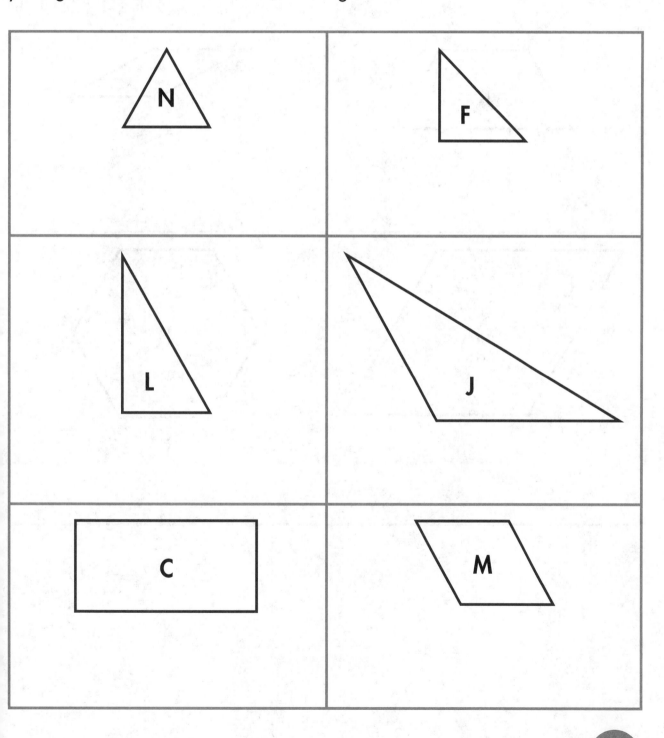

Angles in the Power Polygons (page 2 of 3)

Label each angle with its measure. Explain how you figured out the measure of each angle.

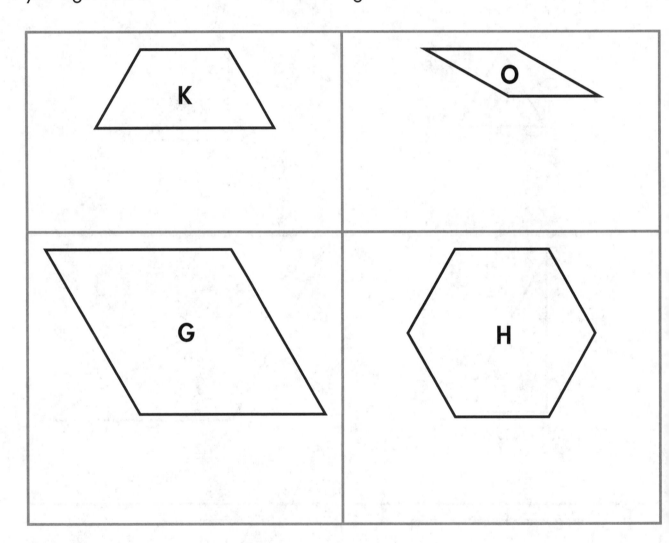

Measuring Polygons

Angles in the Power Polygons (page 3 of 3)

Use the information you found about angle measures on pages 17 and 18 to help you answer these questions.

1. Look at Power Polygon N. What is the sum of all three angles in this triangle?

2. If you add up the angles in the other Power Polygon triangles, will you find the same sum? Why or why not? (First write your prediction, and then check to see whether you are right.)

3. Find the sums of the angles in each of the quadrilaterals in the Power Polygons. What do you notice?

4. Look at the sums of the angles in the triangles and compare them to the sums of the angles in the quadrilaterals. What do you notice? Why do you think this is?

Quadrilateral Categories

> **NOTE** Students identify quadrilaterals and then categorize them by type.
>
> **SMH** 96–98

1. Circle all the shapes that are quadrilaterals.

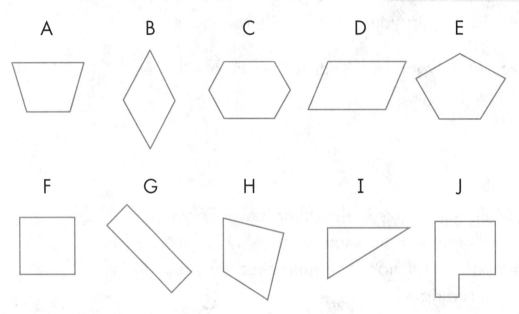

A   B   C   D   E

F   G   H   I   J

2. Put each circled quadrilateral in the following categories. Remember, shapes can be in more than one category!

   These quadrilaterals are parallelograms. _____

   These quadrilaterals are rectangles. _____

   These quadrilaterals are rhombuses. _____

3. Which of the quadrilaterals that you circled have angles that are greater than 90°? _____

Ongoing Review

4. Which quadrilateral is **not** a parallelogram?

   A.   **B.**    **C.**   **D.**

Which Is Greater? Part 1

Solve the following problems. Show how you determined your answers.

NOTE Students compare pairs of fractions and explain how they know which one is larger.

SMH **50–51**

1. Which is greater? $\dfrac{6}{10}$ or $\dfrac{4}{5}$

2. Which is greater? $\dfrac{3}{8}$ or $\dfrac{5}{10}$

3. Which is greater? $1\dfrac{2}{3}$ or $1\dfrac{3}{4}$

4. Which is greater? $\dfrac{6}{5}$ or $1\dfrac{1}{4}$

Multiplying to Make 60 and 90

Find as many ways as you can to multiply whole numbers to make each product.

NOTE Students find multiplication combinations with two factors and with more than two factors for 60 and for 90.

SMH 23–24

1. Multiplying to make 60

Ways to multiply with two factors:	Ways to multiply with more than two factors:

2. Multiplying to make 90

Ways to multiply with two factors:	Ways to multiply with more than two factors:

Ongoing Review

3. Which multiplication combination equals 150?

A. $10 \times 5 \times 10$

C. $25 \times 2 \times 3$

B. $75 \times 2 \times 10$

D. $10 \times 5 \times 5$

Which Is Greater? Part 2

Solve the following problems. Show how you
determined your answers.

NOTE Students compare pairs
of fractions and explain how
they know which one is larger.

SMH 50–51

1. Which is greater? $\frac{3}{4}$ or $\frac{5}{6}$

2. Which is greater? $\frac{4}{10}$ or $\frac{3}{8}$

3. Which is greater? $1\frac{5}{8}$ or $1\frac{2}{3}$

4. Which is greater? $\frac{4}{3}$ or $1\frac{3}{8}$

Follow the Rules

Circle the shape that follows
each set of rules.

NOTE Students practice identifying
properties of polygons.

 95–101

1. • It has 3 sides.
   • It has 1 right angle.
   • It has 2 sides the same length.

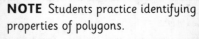

2. • It has exactly one pair of parallel sides.
   • No 2 of the angles are the same size.

3. • It has fewer than 4 sides.
   • It has 1 obtuse angle.
   • It has 2 angles that are the same size.

4. • It has 5 sides.
   • It has 2 right angles.
   • It has exactly 1 pair of parallel sides.

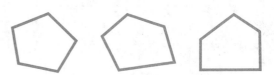

5. • It has exactly 2 pairs of parallel sides.
   • It has 0 right angles.
   • The sides are not all the same length.

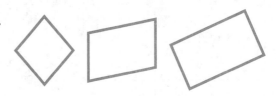

Ongoing Review

6. Crystal ran 9.6 miles each week. How many miles did
   she run in two weeks?

   A. 4.8 mi   **B.** 18.12 mi   **C.** 18.2 mi   **D.** 19.2 mi

© Pearson Education 5

Measuring Polygons

Building a Sequence of Squares

1. Use square tiles to build squares of different sizes. Find the perimeter and area of each square. If you have enough time, make additional squares, and write their measurements in the blanks.

Dimensions of Square	Perimeter	Area
1 inch by 1 inch		
2 inches by 2 inches		
3 inches by 3 inches		
4 inches by 4 inches		
5 inches by 5 inches		
6 inches by 6 inches		
7 inches by 7 inches		

2. What patterns do you see? Make a list of observations about the squares, about their perimeters, or about their areas. Write your observations below. Use a separate sheet of paper if necessary.

Area and Perimeter Fractions and Percents

NOTE Students solve fraction and percent problems involving perimeter and area.

SMH **40–41, 102**

Solve the following problems. Show or explain how you determined your answers.

The students in Ms. Jackson's class built rectangles with color tiles.

1. Felix built a 4 inch by 8 inch rectangle.

    a. What is the perimeter of Felix's rectangle? _____

    b. The perimeter of Hana's rectangle is $\frac{2}{3}$ as long as the perimeter of Felix's. What is the perimeter of Hana's rectangle? _____

    c. What is the area of Felix's rectangle? _____

    d. The area of Martin's rectangle is 25% of the area of Felix's. What is the area of Martin's rectangle? _____

Ongoing Review

2. What do you notice about the area of the rectangles below?

    Which rectangle has the longest perimeter?

    A.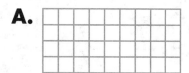

    B.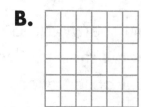

    C.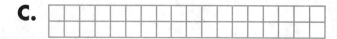

True or False?

Decide whether these statements are true
or false. Circle TRUE or FALSE. Explain
your reasoning.

NOTE Students compare fractions
and percents of different numbers.

SMH 48–49, 50–51

Remember, > means greater than.   Example: 3 > 2
$\qquad$ < means less than. $\qquad$ Example: 2 < 3

1. $\frac{3}{4}$ of 80 > $\frac{2}{3}$ of 120 $\qquad$ TRUE $\qquad$ FALSE

2. $\frac{1}{4}$ of 36 = $\frac{1}{2}$ of 18 $\qquad$ TRUE $\qquad$ FALSE

3. 75% of 200 < 75% of 260 $\qquad$ TRUE $\qquad$ FALSE

Doubling Squares (page 1 of 2)

Use your answers on page 27, *Building a Sequence of Squares,* to answer these questions about how the area of the squares changes.

Record the areas of the following squares:

1. Area of 2-inch square _____

Area of 4-inch square _____

2. Area of 3-inch square _____

Area of 6-inch square _____

3. When you double the sides of the square, how does the area of the larger square change?

4. Why does the area change in this way? Use drawings or other representations to show why this change occurs and explain your thinking.

Doubling Squares (page 2 of 2)

Use your answers on page 27, *Building a Sequence of Squares,* to answer these questions about how the perimeter of the squares changes.

Record the perimeters of the following squares:

5. Perimeter of 2-inch square _____

     Perimeter of 4-inch square _____

6. Perimeter of 3-inch square _____

     Perimeter of 6-inch square _____

7. When you double the sides of the square, how does the perimeter of the larger square change?

8. Why does the perimeter change in this way? Use drawings or other representations to show why this change occurs and explain your thinking.

Which Combination Is Greater?

Solve the following problems. Show how you determined your answers.

NOTE Students add fractions and compare sums to determine which combination is larger.

SMH **50–51, 52–53**

1. Which is greater? $\frac{1}{2} + \frac{1}{6}$ or $\frac{1}{4} + \frac{3}{8}$

2. Which is greater? $\frac{5}{6} + \frac{2}{3}$ or $\frac{9}{10} + \frac{3}{5}$

3. Which is greater? $\frac{3}{4} + \frac{1}{6} + \frac{1}{3}$ or $\frac{5}{8} + \frac{1}{2} + \frac{1}{4}$

4. Which is greater? $\frac{7}{12} + \frac{1}{12} + \frac{1}{6}$ or $\frac{1}{8} + \frac{3}{4}$

Category Search

Some shapes fit many categories. For each shape, write the letters of every category to which it belongs.

NOTE Students classify triangles and quadrilaterals.

SMH 95, 96–98

Categories

A square	**D** trapezoid	**G** equilateral	**J** right
B rectangle	**E** parallelogram	**H** isosceles	**K** obtuse
C rhombus	**F** quadrilateral	**I** scalene	**L** acute

1. _____

2. _____

3. _____

4. _____

5. _____

6. _____

7. _____

8. _____

9. _____

A Sequence of Rectangles (page 1 of 2)

Build or draw the sequence of rectangles shown in the
table below. Record the perimeter and area for each one.
Note that each increase refers to the original rectangle.
For example, you should build or draw shape 4 so that
its sides are the sides of the original rectangle (3-inch x
4-inch) increased 4 times.

	Dimensions of Rectangle	Perimeter	Area
1. Original	3 inches x 4 inches		
2. All sides x 2			
3. All sides x 3			
4. All sides x 4			
5. All sides x 5			
6. All sides x 6			

7. Imagine a rectangle that has all sides x 10. Predict the
following measurements.

Dimensions: _____   Perimeter: _____   Area: _____

Explain your thinking.

A Sequence of Rectangles (page 2 of 2)

8. Consider pairs of rectangles where the dimensions are doubled (rectangles with all sides x 2 and all sides x 4, or those with all sides x 3 and all sides x 6). What happens to the perimeter when you double each of the dimensions of a rectangle?

9. Consider the same pairs of rectangles as above. What happens to the area?

10. Did perimeter and area of rectangles change in the same way it did for squares? Explain your thinking.

In Between Problems

Alex and Shandra are working together to play a perfect game in which they place all of the cards. Write Alex's and Shandra's fractions in the blank cards in the game to show how they can all fit.

> **NOTE** Students practice ordering fractions in a round of "In Between."
>
> **SMH** 50–51, G10

Alex's cards:

| $\frac{3}{10}$ | $\frac{1}{2}$ | $\frac{7}{8}$ | $\frac{9}{10}$ | $\frac{1}{5}$ |

Shandra's cards:

| $\frac{3}{4}$ | $\frac{3}{5}$ | $\frac{3}{8}$ | $\frac{1}{8}$ | $\frac{7}{10}$ |

Game:

| 10% | | | | | 50% | | | | | 90% |

Growing Rectangles

Record the dimensions, perimeter, and area of this rectangle in the table below. Draw rectangles with dimensions twice as long, three times as long, and so on, of the original rectangle. Record the perimeter and area of each one. (Each tile is a 1-inch square.)

NOTE Students find the perimeter and area of a sequence of related rectangles.

SMH 102

	Dimensions of Rectangle	Perimeter	Area
1. Original			
2. All sides x 2			
3. All sides x 3			
4. All sides x 4			
5. All sides x 5			

Rearranging Rectangles

Begin with an 8 by 3 rectangle. Record its perimeter and area in the table below. Imagine cutting the rectangle in half and attaching the two pieces together to make a new rectangle. Record the dimensions, perimeter, and area of the new rectangle in the table below. Repeat this process two more times, and record the information in the table below.

Dimensions	Perimeter	Area
1. 8 inches by 3 inches		
2.		
3.		
4.		

5. What is happening to the area of each rectangle? Why?

6. What is happening to the perimeter of each rectangle? Why?

7. What do you notice about how the shape of the rectangle changes?

More Area and Perimeter Problems

Solve the following problems. Show or explain how you determined your answers.

NOTE Students solve fraction and percent problems involving perimeter and area.

SMH 40–41, 102

1. Janet built a 5-inch by 7-inch rectangle.

   a. What is the perimeter of Janet's rectangle? _____

   b. The perimeter of Olivia's rectangle is 150% as long as Janet's. What is the perimeter of Olivia's rectangle?

   _____

   c. What is the area of Janet's rectangle? _____

   d. The area of Walter's rectangle is $\frac{6}{5}$ the area of Janet's. What is the area of Walter's rectangle?

   _____

2. What do you notice about the perimeters of the rectangles below?

   Which rectangle has the largest area?

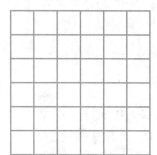

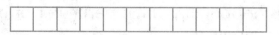

Perimeter Fractions and Percents

NOTE Students solve fraction and percent problems involving perimeter.

SMH 40–41, 102

Solve the following problems. Explain how you determined your answers.

Mrs. Ahmad's fifth-grade students measured the perimeter of some rooms and objects in their school.

1. The perimeter of their classroom is 120 feet. The perimeter of the nurse's office is $\frac{3}{4}$ the perimeter of their classroom.

   What is the perimeter of the nurse's office? _____

2. The perimeter of the rug in their classroom is 38 feet. The perimeter of the classroom door is 50% of that.

   What is the perimeter of the classroom door? _____

3. The perimeter of the office bulletin board is 24 feet. The perimeter of the sandbox in the preschool playground is $1\frac{1}{2}$ times as long.

   What is the perimeter of the sandbox? _____

Fencing a Garden

Ms. Lights' fifth-grade class will plant a garden in the school yard. The garden must be a rectangle, and the principal has given them 30 feet of fencing. Each side of the rectangle has to be a whole number.

Use grid paper, color tiles, or drawings to design at least 4 garden plots that would be enclosed by 30 feet of fence. Find the area for each garden plot.

Attach drawings of your rectangular gardens to this sheet. After you have designed at least four, fill out the table and answer the questions.

	Dimensions	Perimeter	Area
1.		30 feet	
2.		30 feet	
3.		30 feet	
4.		30 feet	
5.		30 feet	
6.		30 feet	
7.		30 feet	

8. What are the dimensions of the rectangle with the largest area?

9. What are the dimensions of the rectangle with the smallest area?

10. What do you notice about the shape of these rectangles?

Measuring Polygons

Rearranging a 16 by 12 Rectangle

Here is a 16-inch by 12-inch rectangle:

Record its perimeter and area in the table below. Imagine cutting the rectangle in half, and attaching the two pieces together to make a new rectangle. Record the dimensions, perimeter, and area of the new rectangle in the table below. Do the same process at least three more times, and record the information in the table below.

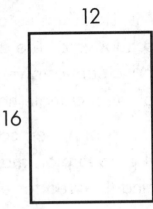

Dimensions	Perimeter	Area
1. 16 inches by 12 inches		
2.		
3.		
4.		
5.		

6. What is happening to the area of each rectangle? Why?

7. What is happening to the perimeter of each rectangle? Why?

8. What do you notice about how the shape of the rectangle changes?

Garden Dimensions

Solve the following problems. Show or explain how you determined your answers.

> **NOTE** Students determine the dimensions of gardens when given the area and the perimeter.
>
> SMH **102**

Alicia, Charles, and Yumiko all planted gardens using 36 feet of fencing for the perimeter.

1. The area of Alicia's garden is 81 square feet. What are the dimensions of her garden?

2. The area of Charles's garden is 45 square feet. What are the dimensions of his garden?

3. The area of Yumiko's garden is 72 square feet. What are the dimensions of her garden?

Ongoing Review

4. Which of the following figures is **not** a regular polygon?

A.   **B.**   **C.**   **D.**

Name the Shaded Portion

Below each 10 x 10 grid, fill in the amount shaded. Write the percent and some equivalent fractions.

NOTE Students use 10 x 10 grids as a model to find fraction and percent equivalents.

 47

1.

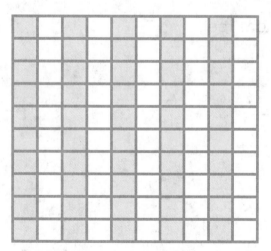

Percent:

Fractions:

2.

Percent:

Fractions:

3.

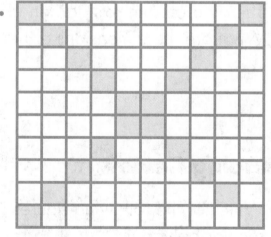

Percent:

Fractions:

4.

Percent:

Fractions:

More Growing Rectangles

Record the dimensions, perimeter, and area of this rectangle in the table below. Draw rectangles with dimensions twice as long, three times as long (and so on) of the original rectangle. Record the perimeter and area of each one. (Each tile is a 1-inch square.)

NOTE Students find the perimeter and area of a sequence of related rectangles.

SMH 102

	Dimensions of Rectangle	Perimeter	Area
1. Original			
2. All sides x 2			
3. All sides x 3			
4. All sides x 4			
5. All sides x 5			

© Pearson Education 3

48 Unit 5

Building Similar Polygons

For each of the Power Polygons shown below, build or draw polygons that are similar. Make the second one with sides two times as long, the third with sides three times as long, the fourth with sides four times as long, and so on.

Polygon	Original	Number of Pieces in Similar (Larger) Shapes			
		2nd	3rd	4th	5th
1. square B					
2. rectangle C					
3. triangle N					
4. triangle J					
5. rhombus M					
6. parallelogram O					

7. Predict how many pieces will be needed for the tenth figure for square B. Explain your thinking.

8. Predict how many pieces will be needed for the tenth figure for triangle N. Explain your thinking.

Seeing Fraction and Percent Equivalents

NOTE Students use 10 x 10 grids as a model to find fraction and percent equivalents.

SMH 47

For each 10 x 10 grid below, shade the portion that represents the given fraction or percent. Write any fraction and percent equivalents.

1.

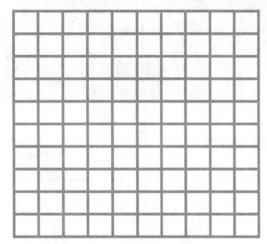

Percent: 25%

Fractions:

2.

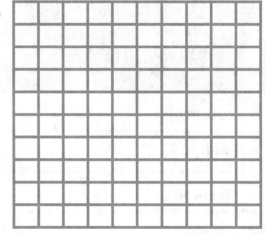

Percent: 30%

Fractions:

3.

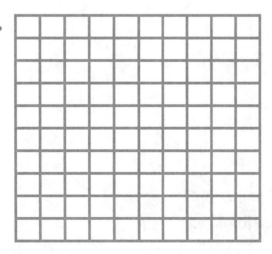

Percent:

Fractions: $\frac{4}{5}$

4.

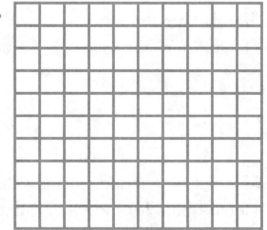

Percent:

Fractions: $\frac{2}{3}$

Measuring Polygons

Homework

Fractions That Add Up to One

Use the clock face to add fractions. Draw a circle around sets of fractions that add up to 1. Use only fractions that are next to each other in a column or row. Some fractions will be used more than once. An example has been done for you.

> **NOTE** Students use fractions on a clock face to add fractions.
>
> **SMH** 52–53

$\dfrac{7}{12}$	$\dfrac{1}{12}$	$\dfrac{1}{3}$
$\dfrac{9}{12}$	$\dfrac{1}{4}$	$\dfrac{5}{6}$
$\dfrac{1}{6}$	$\dfrac{2}{3}$	$\dfrac{2}{12}$

Building Similar Hexagons (page 1 of 2)

1. Draw hexagon H, and then build and draw the second figure, a similar hexagon with each side two times as long as hexagon H. Build the third figure, a similar hexagon with each side three times as long as hexagon H, and draw it on a separate sheet of paper. (For some figures you will need Power Polygon pieces other than H.)

First figure of hexagon H

Second figure of hexagon H

Building Similar Hexagons (page 2 of 2)

2. Look at each hexagon, and record how many of each Power Polygon piece you used to make the second and third hexagon figures:

Second hexagon figure:

Piece	Number Used
triangle N	
rhombus M	
trapezoid K	
hexagon H	

Third hexagon figure:

Piece	Number Used
triangle N	
rhombus M	
trapezoid K	
hexagon H	

3. If the unit of area for each of these similar hexagons is Power Polygon hexagon H, what is the area, in hexagons, of the second figure? Explain how you found your answer.

4. What is the area, in hexagons, of the third figure? Explain how you found your answer.

Similar Shapes on Grids

> **NOTE** Students draw similar shapes on grids with sides two times and three times as long as the sides of the original shapes.
>
> **SMH** 103–104

1. Use the grid to draw a similar shape with sides that are two times as long. Find the area of both shapes.

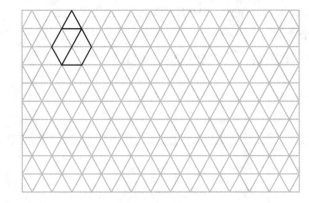

Area of original: _____

Area of new shape: _____

2. Use the grid to draw a similar shape with sides that are three times as long. Count the triangles to find the area of both shapes.

Area of original: _____

Area of new shape: _____

Ongoing Review

3. Which polygon pair is **not** similar?

Drawing Similar Shapes

Use the grids for your drawings.
Find the area of each shape.

> **NOTE** Students first draw similar shapes with sides that are 2 or 3 times as long as the sides of the original shape, and then find the perimeter and area of each shape.
>
> **SMH** 102, 103–104

1. Draw a similar shape with each side that is 2 times as long.

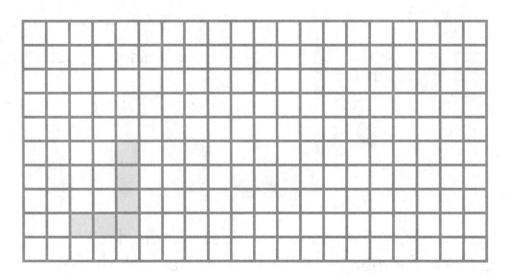

Area of original: _____   Area of new shape: _____

2. Draw a similar shape with each side that is 3 times as long.

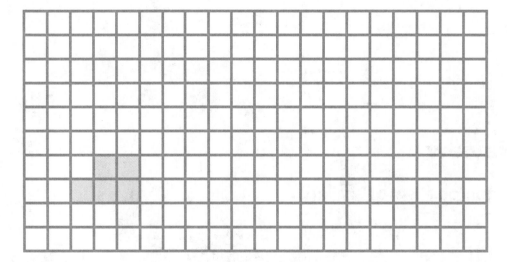

Area of original: _____   Area of new shape: _____

Making a Similarity Poster

Work with a partner for this activity. Use 2–6 of the Power Polygon pieces to build a polygon. Make sure it is not the same size as one of the Power Polygons.

1. Use additional Power Polygons to build figures that are similar to the figure you made. Make one with each side twice as long and one with each side three times as long. Draw each of these figures (the original, the second figure, and the third figure) on a poster.

2. How do the areas of the larger figures compare with the area of your original figure? Use markers or colored pencils to explain your ideas about area on your poster.

3. How do the perimeters of the larger figures compare with the perimeter of your original figure? Use markers or colored pencils to explain your ideas about perimeter on your poster.

School Days

Solve the following problems. Explain how you determined your answers.

NOTE Students solve problems about fractions and percents of a group.

SMH 40–41

1. A class has 24 students.

   a. 50% went to the library. How many students went to the library?

   b. At the same time, 8 of the students helped with the canned food drive. What percent helped with the food drive?

   c. The rest of the students stayed in the classroom to finish their work. What fraction of students stayed in the classroom? What percent is that?

2. Another class has 30 students.

   a. 15 went to the computer lab yesterday. What percent went to the computer lab?

   b. At the same time, 3 out of the 30 students helped in the first grade class. What percent helped in the first grade?

   c. 6 out of the 30 students worked at the writing center. What percent worked at the writing center?

   d. The rest of the students were absent. How many students were absent? What percent of students were absent?

Area Patterns

Count small squares or small triangles
to find the areas.

NOTE Students find the area of pairs of
similar shapes in which one shape has sides
twice as long as the other.

SMH **102, 103–104**

1.

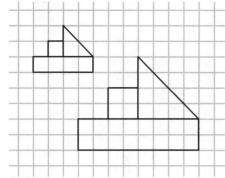

2.

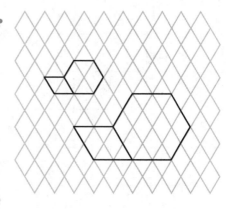

3.

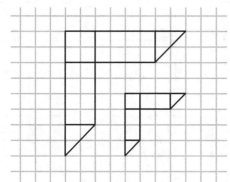

4.

5. In a pair of similar polygons, the polygon with
sides that are two times as long as the other has
an area that is _____ times as large.

Ongoing Review

6. Complete this equation: $\frac{1}{2} + \frac{1}{6} =$ _____

A. 1   **B.** $\frac{2}{3}$ **C.** $\frac{1}{3}$ **D.** $\frac{3}{12}$

Polygon Pairs

Look at each pair of polygons. Are the polygons in each pair similar or not similar? Explain why you think so.

NOTE Students determine whether pairs of polygons are similar or not similar and explain their reasoning.

SMH 103–104

1.

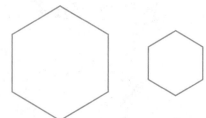

_____

2.

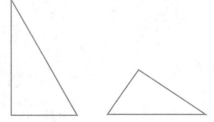

_____

3.

_____

Ongoing Review

4. Which shape is **not** a pentagon?

A. 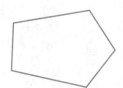 **B.**   **C.** 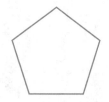 **D.**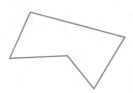

Fraction Problems

Solve these problems, and show or explain how
you solved them.

> **NOTE** Students practice
> adding and subtracting
> fractions.
>
> **SMH** 52–53

1. Mercedes and Zachary made two pans of
   cornbread. They gave $\frac{3}{4}$ of a pan to their
   grandmother. Their family ate $\frac{2}{3}$ of a pan
   for supper. How much cornbread was left?

2. $\frac{5}{8} + \frac{1}{4} + \frac{3}{3} =$ _____

3. $4 - \frac{5}{6} =$ _____

Similar Polygons

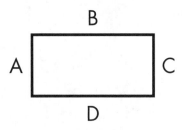

B

A ____ C

D

NOTE Students determine dimension for polygons that are similar by creating a table, and then explain their reasoning.

SMH 103–104

Austin is choosing a pool for his backyard. He has found a design that he likes in the brochure. Austin wants a pool that is similar, but he will enlarge the dimensions to double the size of the pool he chose in the brochure.

1. Use the table to determine the dimensions of his pool. Each side of the pool is doubled. Write the new dimensions for each side in the table.

	Side A	Side B	Side C	Side D
Austin's Pool				
Brochure Pool	4 ft	8 ft	4 ft	8 ft

2. Draw a picture of Austin's pool. Label the dimensions of each side of the pool.

3. Explain why the two pools are similar.

Parrot Fire Kris Northern

"Rather than zoom into the fractal you can zoom into the edge of it and continually find the same pattern repeating itself much like the shoreline of a lake viewed from a plane." – **Kris Northern**

Investigations
IN NUMBER, DATA, AND SPACE®

Student Activity Book

Decimals on Grids and Number Lines

UNIT 6

Decimals on Grids and Number Lines

Investigation 1

Investigation 2

Decimals on Grids and Number Lines

Tenths and Hundredths

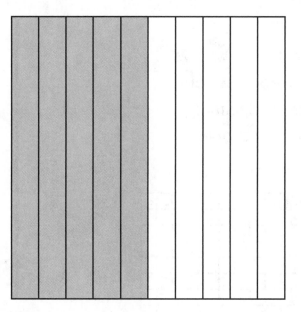
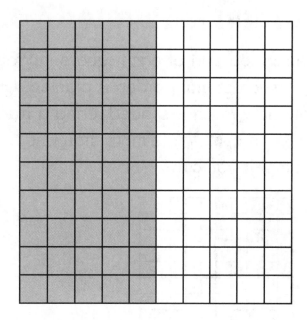

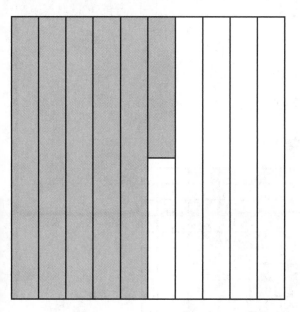
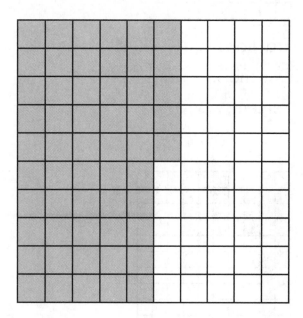

How Much of the Garden Is Planted? (page 1 of 3)

The shaded part of each square in Problems 1–10 shows how much of that garden is planted. Under each square, write how much is shaded, using a fraction, a decimal, and a percent. Write more than one fraction and one decimal if you can.

1.

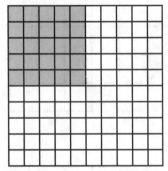

Fractions:

Decimals:

Percent:

2.

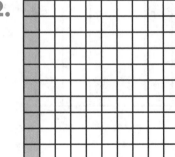

Fractions:

Decimals:

Percent:

3.

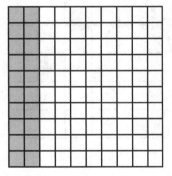

Fractions:

Decimals:

Percent:

4.

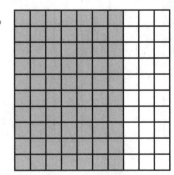

Fractions:

Decimals:

Percent:

How Much of the Garden Is Planted? (page 2 of 3)

5.

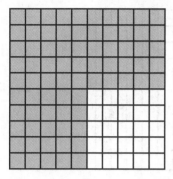

Fractions: _____

Decimals: _____

Percent: _____

6.

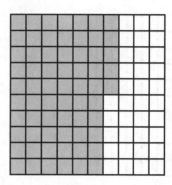

Fractions: _____

Decimals: _____

Percent: _____

7.

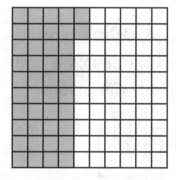

Fractions: _____

Decimals: _____

Percent: _____

8.

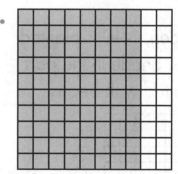

Fractions: _____

Decimals: _____

Percent: _____

Decimals on Grids and Number Lines

How Much of the Garden Is Planted? (page 3 of 3)

9.

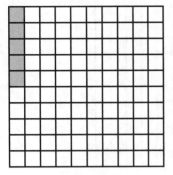

Fractions:

Decimals:

Percent:

10.

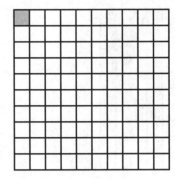

Fractions:

Decimals:

Percent:

11. In this garden, 0.40 is planted with beans. Shade in the part that is planted with beans.

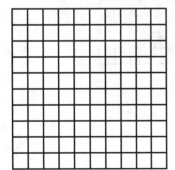

What are other ways you know to write this amount?

12. In this garden, 0.98 is planted with onions. Shade in the part that is planted with onions.

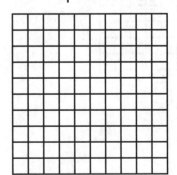

What are other ways you know to write this amount?

How Much Is Shaded?

Look at the shaded part of each square. Under each square, write how much is shaded using a fraction, a decimal, and a percent. Write more than one fraction and one decimal if you can.

NOTE Students identify parts of a square and name them with fractions, percents, and decimals.

SMH 46

1.

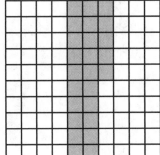

Fractions:

Decimals:

Percent:

2.

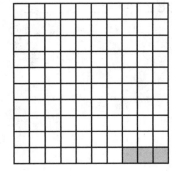

Fractions:

Decimals:

Percent:

3. Shade in 0.80. What are other ways you know to write this amount?

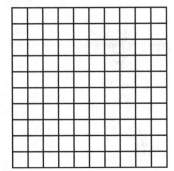

4. Shade in 0.43. What are other ways you know to write this amount?

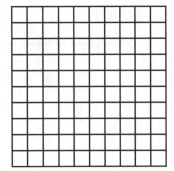

Ongoing Review

5. What is the decimal equivalent of 32%?

A. 0.032   **B.** 0.32   **C.** 3.2   **D.** 32.0

Adding and Subtracting Large Numbers

> **NOTE** Students review adding and subtracting large numbers.
>
> **SMH** 8–9, 10–13

Solve each problem. Your solution should be clear and concise.

1. 9,413 − 5,582 = _____

2.   4,290
   −2,887

3. 10,579 + 8,013 = _____

4.   45,899
   − 6,125

5. 14,002 − 2,995 = _____

Hundredths and Thousandths (page 1 of 2)

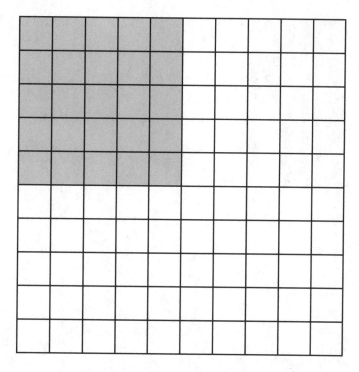

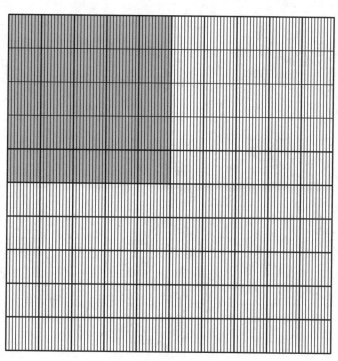

Decimals on Grids and Number Lines

Hundredths and Thousandths (page 2 of 2)

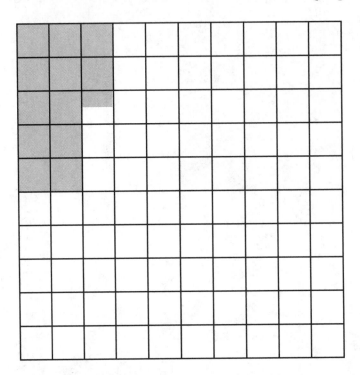

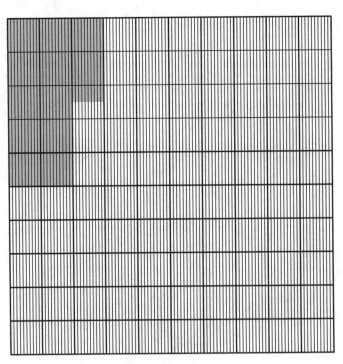

Decimals on Hundredths and Thousandths Grids (page 1 of 6)

Shade in the squares. Write the decimals, fractions, and percent you know for each pair.

1. Shade in 0.75 on each square.

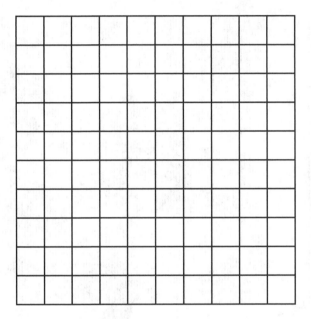
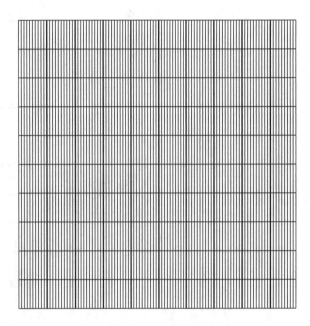

Decimals: 0.75, _____   Decimals: 0.75, _____

Fractions: Fractions:

Percent: Percent:

Decimals on Hundredths and Thousandths Grids (page 2 of 6)

Shade in the squares. Write the decimals, fractions, and percent you know for each pair.

2. Shade in 0.125 on each square.

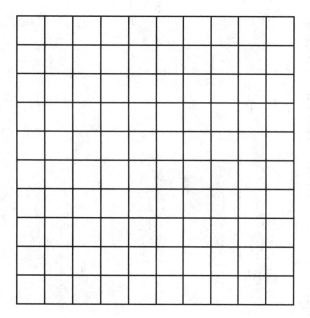

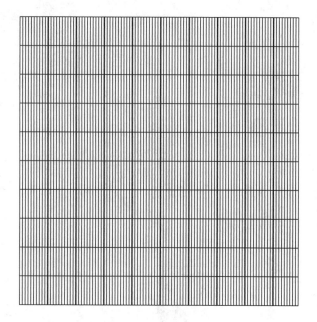

Decimals: 0.125, _____

Fractions:

Percent:

Decimals: 0.125, _____

Fractions:

Percent:

Decimals on Hundredths and Thousandths Grids (page 3 of 6)

Shade in the squares. Write the decimals, fractions, and percent you know for each pair.

3. Shade in 0.3 on each square.

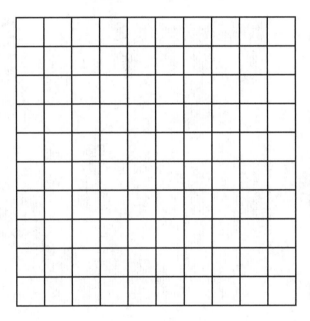

Decimals: 0.3, _____

Fractions:

Percent:

Decimals: 0.3, _____

Fractions:

Percent:

Decimals on Hundredths and Thousandths Grids (page 4 of 6)

Shade in the squares. Write the decimals, fractions, and percent you know for each pair.

4. Shade in 0.15 on each square.

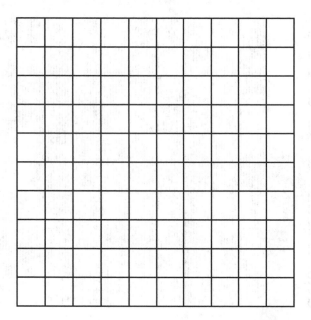 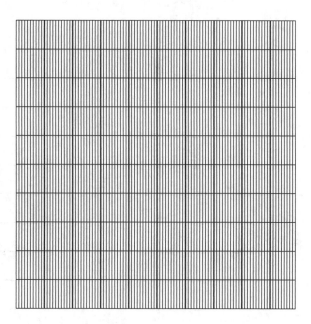

Decimals: 0.15, _____

Fractions:

Percent:

Decimals: 0.15, _____

Fractions:

Percent:

Decimals on Hundredths and Thousandths Grids (page 5 of 6)

Shade in the squares. Write the decimals, fractions, and percent you know for each pair.

5. Shade in 0.78 on each square.

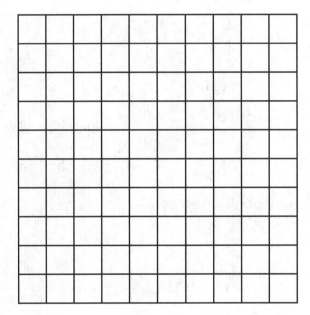

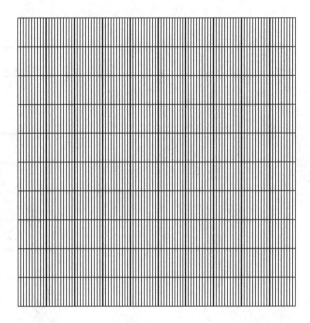

Decimals: 0.78, _____

Fractions:

Percent:

Decimals: 0.78, _____

Fractions:

Percent:

Decimals on Hundredths and Thousandths Grids (page 6 of 6)

Shade in the squares. Write the decimals, fractions, and percent you know for each pair.

6. Shade in 0.625 on each square.

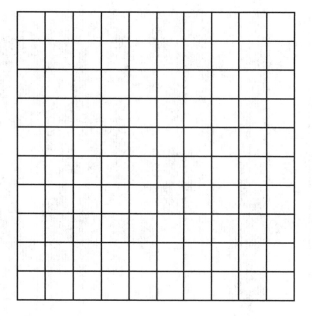   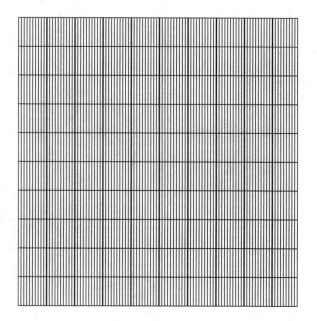

Decimals: 0.625, _____   Decimals: 0.625, _____

Fractions: Fractions:

Percent: Percent:

Matching Shaded Portions

NOTE Students match the shaded portion of the grid with the correct decimal and fractions.

SMH 55–56

1. Match each grid to the fractions and decimals that describe the shaded part of the grid.

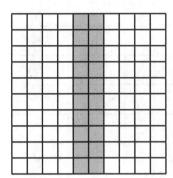 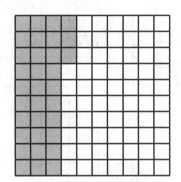 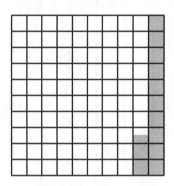

| $\frac{1}{8}$ | 0.2 | 0.33 | $\frac{33}{100}$ | 0.125 | $\frac{200}{1,000}$ | $\frac{125}{1,000}$ |

Ongoing Review

2. Which equation is **not** true?

A. $0.500 = \frac{1}{2}$ **C.** $0.75 = \frac{3}{4}$

B. $\frac{1}{3} = 0.13333$ **D.** $\frac{2}{10} = 20\%$

Decimal Grids

Tenths

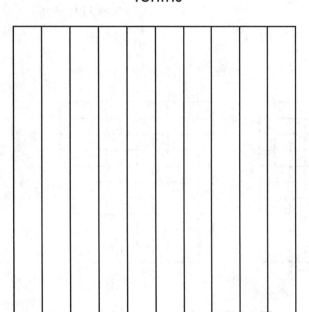

Hundredths

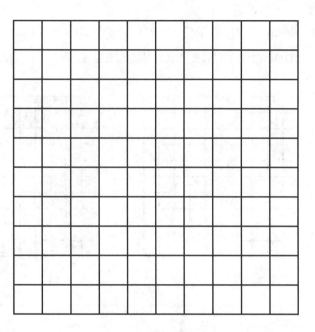

Thousandths

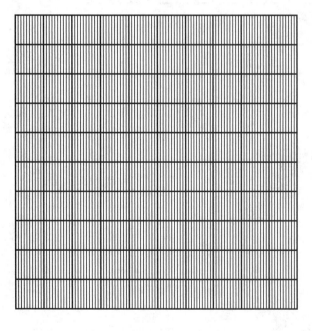

Ten Thousandths

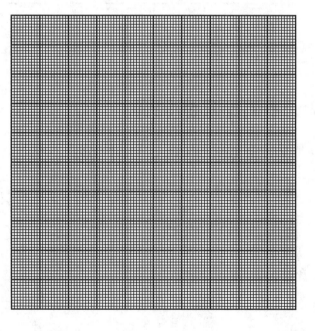

Ordering Decimals

For each number line, deal out five Decimal Cards and mark each decimal on the number line.

1.

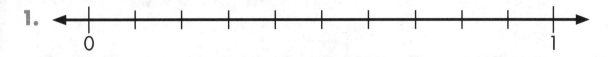

0   1

2.

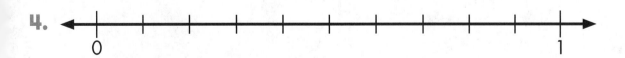

0   1

3.

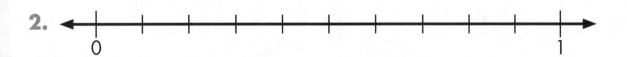

0   1

4.

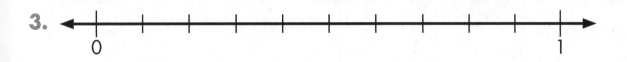

0   1

Decimals on Grids and Number Lines

Solve Two Ways

Solve each problem in two ways.
Show your work clearly.

> **NOTE** Students practice flexibility with solving multiplication problems and use one method to check the other. Use anytime during this unit.
>
> **SMH** 30–32

1. $76 \times 29 =$ _____

First way:	Second way:

2. $58 \times 46 =$ _____

First way:	Second way:

Ongoing Review

3. Which of the following is **true**?

A. $80 \times 10 > 50 \times 20$ **C.** $50 \times 6 < 7 \times 40$

B. $30 \times 70 > 20 \times 100$ **D.** $100 \times 70 < 30 \times 30$

Decimals on Grids and Number Lines

Ordering Precipitation Amounts

NOTE Students practice putting decimals in order.

SMH 61–62

Here are 30-year averages of monthly precipitation for two cities. Put the months in order from the least amount of precipitation per month to the greatest amount. All amounts are recorded in inches.

1. Pueblo, Colorado*

January: 0.32   February: 0.31   March: 0.78   April: 0.88   May: 1.25

Month	Precipitation

2. Bridgeport, Connecticut*

January: 3.24   February: 3.01   March: 3.75   April: 3.96   May: 3.46

Month	Precipitation

*Data are for the years 1961–1990.

© Pearson Education 5

Multiplication Starter Problems

NOTE Students practice flexibility with solving multiplication problems and use one method to check the other.

SMH 30–32

Solve each problem two ways, using the first steps listed below. Show your work clearly.

1. $78 \times 45 =$ _____

Start by solving $80 \times 45 =$	Start by solving $70 \times 40 =$

2. $32 \times 128 =$ _____

Start by solving $32 \times 100 =$	Start by solving $10 \times 128 =$

Ongoing Review

3. Which number is **not** a factor of 300?

A. 25   **B.** 18   **C.** 6   **D.** 4

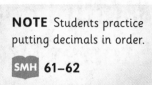

More Precipitation

Here are 30-year averages of monthly precipitation for two cities. Put the months in order, from the least amount of precipitation per month to the greatest amount. All amounts are recorded in inches.

NOTE Students practice putting decimals in order.

SMH 61–62

1. Mobile, Alabama*

January: 4.76 February: 5.46 March: 6.41 April: 4.48 May: 5.74

Month	Precipitation

2. Nome, Alaska*

June: 1.12 July: 2.17 August: 2.71 September: 2.43 October: 1.35

Month	Precipitation

*Data are for the years 1961–1990.

Decimal Problems (page 1 of 3)

Shade in the squares. Write the fraction and percent equivalents below each grid.

1. Shade in 0.5.

2. Shade in 0.295.

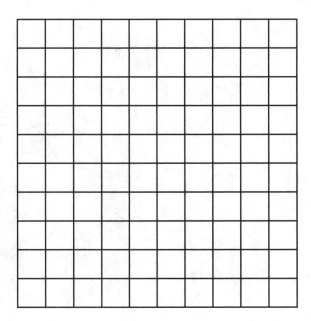

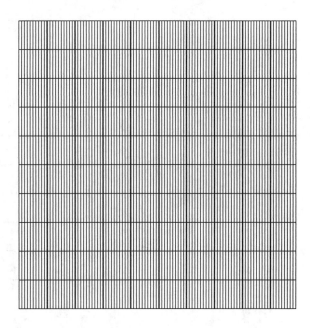

Decimals: 0.5, _____

Fractions:

Percent:

Decimals: 0.295, _____

Fractions:

Percent:

Decimal Problems (page 2 of 3)

Shade in the squares. Write the fraction and percent
equivalents below each grid.

3. Shade in 0.83.

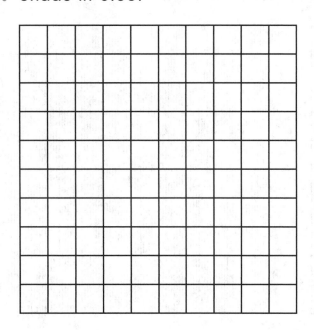

Decimals: 0.83, _____

Fractions:

Percent:

4. Shade in 0.150.

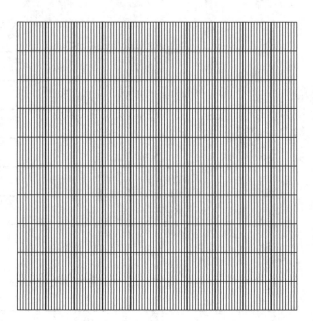

Decimals: 0.150, _____

Fractions:

Percent:

Decimal Problems (page 3 of 3)

Solve the following decimal problems in story context.

5. Mitch and Hana have gardens that are the same size.
Mitch planted 0.250 of his garden with tomatoes.
Hana planted $\frac{3}{8}$ of her garden with tomatoes.
Who planted more of the garden with tomatoes?
Explain how you found your answer.

6. Mitch planted 0.6 of his garden with corn.
Hana planted 0.505 of her garden with corn.
Who planted more of the garden with corn?
Explain how you found your answer.

7. Mitch also planted 0.15 of his garden with peppers.
Which part of his garden is the largest, the part with
tomatoes, the part with corn, or the part with peppers?

The Decimal Trail

Markers show where these decimals are located along the trail.

NOTE Students practice ordering decimals from least to greatest.

SMH 61–62

0.123; 0.601; 0.661; 0.79; 0.5; 0.165; 0.400; 0.245; 0.75; 0.333; 0.625

1. Write the decimals on the marker.

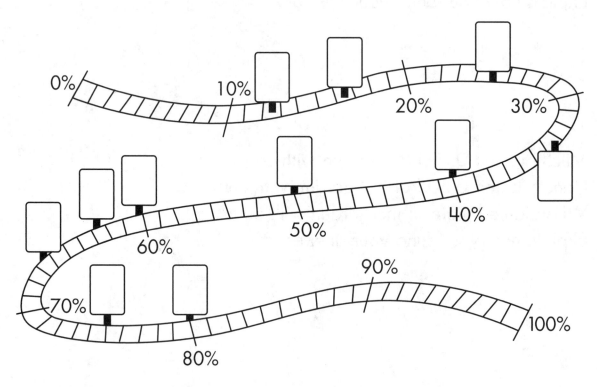

Ongoing Review

2. Which sentence is **not** true?

   A. $0.15 < 0.015$ **C.** $0.633 = \frac{633}{1,000}$

   B. $2.275 > 1.355$ **D.** $0.125 < 0.25$

Swim Meet: 100-Meter Freestyle

For each race below, place the times in order from fastest to slowest. Times are recorded in seconds (56.75 is fifty-six and 75 hundredths seconds).

NOTE Students practice ordering decimals by using information from the 2004 swimming U.S. Summer National Championships.

SMH 61–62

100-Meter Freestyle: Women*

Name	Time
Kara Denby	56.75
Kate Dwelley	56.63
Tanica Jamison	55.96
Shelly Ripple Johnston	57.02
Danielle Townsend	56.65

Place	Time
1st	55.96
2nd	56.63
3rd	56.65
4th	56.75
5th	57.02

100-Meter Freestyle: Men*

Name	Time
Garrett Weber-Gale	49.91
Antoine Galavtine	50.54
Scott Tucker	50.14
Ryan Verlatti	50.54
Sebastien Bodet	50.50

Place	Time
1st	49.91
2nd	50.14
3rd	50.50
4th	50.54
5th	50.54

*Source: www.usaswimming.org

Smaller to Larger

Arrange the decimals on the grid so that each row from left to right and each column from top to bottom is in increasing order.

NOTE Students practice ordering decimals from least to greatest, both horizontally and vertically, on a grid.

SMH 61–62, G11

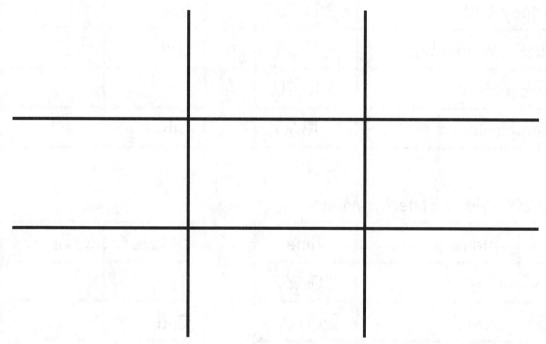

Ongoing Review

Circle the decimal number with the smallest value.

A. 0.5   **B.** 0.050   **C.** 0.005   **D.** 0.1

Swim Meet: 200-Meter Butterfly

For each race below, place the times in order from fastest to slowest. Times are recorded in minutes and seconds (2:13.23 is 2 minutes, 13 and 23 hundredths seconds).

NOTE Students practice ordering decimals by using information from the 2004 swimming U.S. Summer National Championships.

SMH 61–62

200-Meter Butterfly: Women*

Name	Time
Kailey Morris	2:16.76
Courtney Eads	2:11.73
Kimberly Vandenberg	2:11.08
Amanda Sims	2:16.20
Kristen Hastrup	2:13.95

Place	Time
1st	2.11.08
2nd	2.11.73
3rd	2.13.95
4th	
5th	

200-Meter Butterfly: Men*

Name	Time
Michael Klueh	2:00.67
William Stovall	2:00.03
John Abercrombie	2:00.66
Juan Valdivieso	2:02.61
Wade Kelley	2:01.26

Place	Time
1st	
2nd	
3rd	
4th	
5th	

*Source: www.usaswimming.org

Decimals on Grids and Number Lines

Win/Loss Records

Find the record for each set of teams below, and rank them
from the team with the best record to the team with the
worst record. Then, write an approximate winning
percentage for each of the teams.

1.

Team	Wins	Losses	Record* (decimal)	Rank	Winning Percentage
Bluebirds	20	5			
Cardinals	12	12			
Orioles	16	9			
Penguins	10	15			
Robins	19	6			

2.

Team	Wins	Losses	Record* (decimal)	Rank	Winning Percentage
Cheetahs	20	20			
Leopards	10	30			
Jaguars	18	23			
Tigers	35	5			
Lions	34	5			

*Write the record in thousandths. For example, if a team has 16 wins and
10 losses, the calculator would display 0.6153846. Write 0.615. If a team
has 9 wins and 1 loss, the calculator would display 0.9. Write 0.900.

Factors of 360 and 600

Find all the ways to multiply to make each product, using whole numbers. First, find ways with two numbers, and then find ways to multiply with more than two numbers.

NOTE Students practice finding multiplication expressions with two numbers and with more than two numbers that are equal to 360 and 600.

SMH 18, 23–24

Multiplying to Make 360

Ways to multiply with two numbers:	Ways to multiply with more than two numbers:
Example: 36 × 10	Example: 6 × 6 × 10

Multiplying to Make 600

Ways to multiply with two numbers:	Ways to multiply with more than two numbers:

Swim Meet: 50-Meter Freestyle

For each race below, place the times in order from fastest to slowest. Times are recorded in seconds (26.21 is 26 and 21 hundredths seconds).

NOTE Students practice ordering decimals by using information from the 2004 swimming U.S. Summer National Championships.

SMH 61–62

50-Meter Freestyle: Women*

Name	Time
Andrea Georoff	26.19
Tanica Jamison	26.11
Danielle Townsend	26.16
Katrina Radke	26.19
Brooke Bishop	26.10

Place	Time
1st	
2nd	
3rd	
4th	
5th	

50-Meter Freestyle: Men*

Name	Time
Randall Bal	22.75
Cullen Jones	23.08
David Maitre	22.86
Mark Whittington	23.04
Antoine Galavtine	23.03

Place	Time
1st	
2nd	
3rd	
4th	
5th	

*Source: www.usaswimming.org

34

Fraction-to-Decimal Division Table

$\frac{N}{D}$	1	2	3	4	5	6	7	8	9	10	11	12
1												
2												
3												
4												
5												
6												
7												
8												
9												
10												
11												
12												

Solving Division Problems

NOTE Students practice solving division problems.

SMH **38–39**

1. **a.** Write a story problem that can be represented by 390 ÷ 26.

   b. Solve 390 ÷ 26. Show your solution clearly.

2. **a.** Write a story problem that can be represented by $19\overline{)665}$.

   b. Solve $19\overline{)665}$. Show your solution clearly.

Ongoing Review

3. Which number is **not** a multiple of 15?

   A. 250   **B.** 300   **C.** 345   **D.** 600

Who's Winning?

Find the record for each set of teams below, and rank them from the team with the best record to the team with the worst record. Then, write an approximate winning percentage for each of the teams.

1.

Team	Wins	Losses	Record* (decimal)	Rank	Winning Percentage
Dolphins	15	34			
Guppies	38	11			
Marlins	25	25			
Sharks	24	25			
Swordfish	40	10			

2.

Team	Wins	Losses	Record* (decimal)	Rank	Winning Percentage
Wolves	98	27			
Coyotes	63	61			
Bobcats	96	28			
Wildcats	62	62			
Tigers	60	64			

*Write the record in thousandths. For example, if a team has 16 wins and 10 losses, the calculator would display 0.6153846. Write 0.615. If a team has 9 wins and 1 loss, the calculator would display 0.9. Write 0.900.

Division Practice

Solve each division problem below. Then write the related multiplication combination.

NOTE Students review division problems that are related to the multiplication combinations they know.

SMH 14, 25–29

Division Problem	Multiplication Combination
1. 7)42	____ × ____ = ____
2. 72 ÷ 6 = ____	____ × ____ = ____
3. 8)48	____ × ____ = ____
4. 108 ÷ 9 = ____	____ × ____ = ____
5. 60 ÷ 12 = ____	____ × ____ = ____
6. 36 ÷ 6 = ____	____ × ____ = ____
7. 12)96	____ × ____ = ____
8. 63 ÷ 7 = ____	____ × ____ = ____
9. 72 ÷ 9 = ____	____ × ____ = ____
10. 9)54	____ × ____ = ____

Fraction, Decimal, and Percent Equivalents

Fill in each box with the equivalent fraction, decimal, or percent.

NOTE Students find equivalent fractions, decimals, and percents. Students will know some of these equivalents easily and may use a calculator to figure out others.

SMH 59–60

Fraction	Decimal	Percent
$\frac{1}{3}$		$33\frac{1}{3}\%$
$5\frac{1}{4}$		
$\frac{2}{3}$		
	2.5	250%
$\frac{1}{6}$		
		75%
$\frac{8}{10}$		
	0.375	

Teams

Solve the problems below. Your work should
be clear enough that anyone looking at it will
know how you solved the problem.

NOTE Students practice solving
multiplication and division
problems in story contexts.

SMH 14, 30–32, 38–39

1. There are 44 teams in the youth football league.
   Each team has 28 players. How many football
   players are there?

2. 438 people signed up for a city soccer league.
   The league places 15 people on each team.
   How many teams are there?

3. There are 544 students at Field Day, organized into
   34 teams. How many students are on each team?

4. There are 107 teams and 19 people on each team.
   How many people are on teams?

Which Is Greater?

> **NOTE** Students practice comparing decimals and fractions.
>
> SMH 59–60, 61–62

Solve the problems below and show or explain how you determined the answer.

1. Which is greater?   0.15   or $\frac{1}{5}$

2. Which is greater? $\frac{7}{8}$ or   0.95

3. A pudding recipe calls for 0.355 liter of milk. Tavon has 0.5 liter of milk at home. Does he have enough milk for the pudding recipe?

4. Tavon put 4.63 ounces of chocolate in his pudding. Nora put 4.625 ounces in her pudding. Who put more chocolate in the pudding?

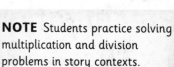

Collections

Solve each of the following problems. Show your work clearly. Be sure to answer the question posed in the problem.

> **NOTE** Students practice solving multiplication and division problems in story contexts.
>
> **SMH** 14, 30–32, 38–39

1. Walter buys stickers in packages of 36 for his sticker collection. Last year he bought 97 packages of stickers. How many stickers did he buy?

2. **a.** Zachary wants to sell his marble collection at a yard sale. He has 744 marbles and he wants to put them into bags with 24 marbles in each bag. How many bags of marbles will he have?

   b. If Zachary sells each bag of marbles for $14 at the yard sale, how much money will he earn by selling his marble collection?

3. **a.** Georgia has 580 sport cards in her collection, which she keeps in a binder that holds 32 cards on a page. How many pages are filled with cards?

   b. Georgia paid $1.50 for each sport card. How much did she spend to buy all of the cards in her collection?

Decimals on Grids and Number Lines

Precipitation in the Desert

These are 30-year averages of monthly precipitation for Phoenix and Las Vegas. For each city, put the months in order, from the least amount of precipitation per month to the greatest amount. All amounts are recorded in inches.

> **NOTE** Students practice ordering decimals.
>
> **SMH** 61–62

1. Phoenix, Arizona*

   January: 0.67;   February: 0.68;   April: 0.22;   May: 0.12;   June: 0.13

Month	Precipitation

2. Las Vegas, Nevada*

   August: 0.49;   September: 0.28;   October: 0.21;   November: 0.43;
   December: 0.38

Month	Precipitation

*Data are for the years 1961–1990.

The Jeweler's Gold

In your small groups, do the following:

1. Answer the question below. Everyone should agree on what the answer is.

2. Create a poster showing your answer, and explain how you added the numbers together.

Janet is a jeweler. When she makes new jewelry or redesigns jewelry, she is often left with small pieces of gold. At the end of one day of work, Janet had pieces of gold that weighed 0.3 gram, 1.14 grams, and 0.085 gram. How much gold did Janet have left?

Closest Estimate

NOTE Students practice strategies for estimating products.

Each problem below has a choice of three estimates. Which one do you think is closest? Choose the closest estimate without solving the problem. Circle it. Then write about why you think this estimate is the closest.

1. The closest estimate for 83 × 29 is:

   2,000   2,400   2,800

   I think this is the closest because:

2. The closest estimate for 69 × 38 is:

   1,800   2,200   2,600

   I think this is the closest because:

3. The closest estimate for 26 × 211 is:

   4,500   5,000   5,500

   I think this is the closest because:

4. The closest estimate for 496 × 18 is:

   900   9,000   90,000

   I think this is the closest because:

5. Choose one or more of the problems above and, on a separate sheet of paper, solve it to get an exact answer. Show your solution with equations. Did you choose the closest estimate?

Decimals In Between Problems

NOTE Students practice ordering decimals in this sample round of the "Decimals In Between" game.

SMH 61–62

Talisha and Avery are working together to play a perfect game in which they place all of the cards. They have each played one card. Write Talisha's and Avery's decimals in the blank cards in the game below to show how every card can be played.

Talisha's cards:

| 0.475 | 0.325 | 0.25 | 0.95 | 0.75 |

Avery's cards:

| 0.3 | 0.05 | 0.55 | 0.8 | 0.65 |

Game:

| 0 | 0.025 | | | | | | | 0.5 | | | | | | 0.975 | 1 |

Decimals on Grids and Number Lines

Adding Decimals (page 1 of 2)

For each problem below, deal out five Decimal Cards and write them on the lines. Determine which three of the decimals have the greatest value, and add them. Show your work clearly.

1. Decimals: _____ _____ _____ _____ _____

   Addition problem: _____ + _____ + _____ = _____

2. Decimals: _____ _____ _____ _____ _____

   Addition problem: _____ + _____ + _____ = _____

3. Decimals: _____ _____ _____ _____ _____

   Addition problem: _____ + _____ + _____ = _____

Adding Decimals (page 2 of 2)

For each problem below, deal out five Decimal Cards and write them on the lines. Determine which three of the decimals have the greatest value, and add them. Show your work clearly.

4. Decimals: _____ _____ _____ _____ _____

Addition problem: _____ + _____ + _____ = _____

5. Decimals: _____ _____ _____ _____ _____

Addition problem: _____ + _____ + _____ = _____

6. Decimals: _____ _____ _____ _____ _____

Addition problem: _____ + _____ + _____ = _____

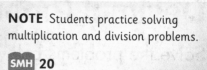

Mystery Tower

This is the top part of Janet's Multiple Tower. Answer these questions about her tower.

NOTE Students practice solving multiplication and division problems.

SMH 20

1. What number did Janet count by? How do you know?

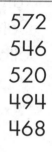

| 572 |
| 546 |
| 520 |
| 494 |
| 468 |

2. How many numbers are in Janet's tower so far? How do you know?

3. Write a multiplication equation that represents how many numbers are in Janet's Multiple Tower:

   _____ × _____ = _____

4. What is the 10th multiple in Janet's tower?

5. Imagine that Janet adds more multiples to her tower.

   a. What would be the 30th multiple in her tower? How do you know?

   b. What would be the 32nd multiple in her tower? How do you know?

Decimal Problems (page 1 of 2)

Solve the problems below, showing your work clearly.

1. Shandra is preparing to run in a race. On Tuesday she ran 1.5 miles, on Thursday she ran 2.9 miles, and on Saturday she ran 2 miles. How many miles did she run altogether?

2. Mercedes finds two small pieces of gold in her jewelry tray. One weighs 0.48 gram and the other weighs 0.55 gram. How much gold did Mercedes find?

3. $1.29 + 3.654 =$ _____

4. Joshua is preparing for a race. On Monday he ran 1.75 miles, and on Wednesday he ran 1.6 miles. How many total miles did he run?

5. $0.98 + 0.05 + 1.06 =$ _____

Decimal Problems (page 2 of 2)

Find the total amount of precipitation for the 3 months in the tables below, showing your work clearly. All amounts are recorded in inches.*

6.

City	Jan.	Feb.	May	Total
Sacramento, California	3.73	2.87	0.27	

7.

City	Sept.	Oct.	Nov.	Total
Helena, Montana	1.15	0.6	0.48	

8.

City	Jan.	Feb.	March	Total
Lincoln, Nebraska	0.54	0.72	2.09	

9.

City	Jan.	Feb.	March	Total
Harrisburg, Pennsylvania	2.84	2.93	3.28	

10.

City	June	July	Sept.	Total
Austin, Texas	3.72	2.04	3.3	

*Data are monthly averages for the years 1961–1990.

Gymnastics: Women's All-Around Scores

Here are the scores of six female gymnasts from the 2004 Olympics in Athens, Greece.

NOTE Students practice adding decimals to thousandths and ordering decimals. Students should have thousandths grids available.

SMH **61–62, 63–65**

Name	Floor Exercise	Vault	Total Score
Nan Zhang	9.600	9.325	
Kwang Sun Pyon	8.900	8.525	
Elena Gomez	9.462	9.150	
Carly Patterson	9.712	9.375	
Daniela Sofroni	9.537	9.412	
Katy Lennon	8.925	9.262	

1. Find each gymnast's total score for Floor Exercise plus Vault and record it on the chart.

2. Rank the gymnasts from the highest to the lowest score in Floor Exercise.

Ongoing Review

3. What is the total of the top three vault scores?

A. 28.112   **B.** 27.112   **C.** 27.102   **D.** 27.002

Fill Two Problems

Nora and Charles are playing *Fill Two*.
Answer these questions about their game.

NOTE Students practice adding decimals with these problems from the game "Fill Two."

SMH **63–65**

1. On her first grid, Nora played 0.35, 0.425, and 0.075. How much of her first grid did Nora fill in? Show how you got the sum.

2. On her second grid, Nora played 0.6 and 0.25. How much of her second grid did Nora fill in? Show how you got the sum.

3. On his first grid, Charles played 0.175, 0.5, and 0.125. How much of his first grid did Charles fill in? Show how you got the sum.

4. On his second grid, Charles played 0.25, 0.65, and 0.05. How much of his second grid did Charles fill in? Show how you got the sum.

5. Who won the game? (Remember that the winner is the one with the sum of both grids closest to 2.) Show how you got your answer.

Close to 1 Recording Sheet

(Use only the number of blanks you need.)

Score

Round 1: ____ + ____ + ____ + ____ + ____ = ____ ____

Round 2: ____ + ____ + ____ + ____ + ____ = ____ ____

Round 3: ____ + ____ + ____ + ____ + ____ = ____ ____

Round 4: ____ + ____ + ____ + ____ + ____ = ____ ____

Round 5: ____ + ____ + ____ + ____ + ____ = ____ ____

Final Score: _____

Score

Round 1: ____ + ____ + ____ + ____ + ____ = ____ ____

Round 2: ____ + ____ + ____ + ____ + ____ = ____ ____

Round 3: ____ + ____ + ____ + ____ + ____ = ____ ____

Round 4: ____ + ____ + ____ + ____ + ____ = ____ ____

Round 5: ____ + ____ + ____ + ____ + ____ = ____ ____

Final Score: _____

Decimal Double Compare Recording Sheet

Choose five different rounds from *Decimal Double Compare* and record on this sheet. Use the <, >, or = signs between the cards. Write the sum of each pair below the cards.

1. Your cards: Partner's cards:

◯

_____ _____   _____ _____

Sum: _____   Sum: _____

2. Your cards: Partner's cards:

◯

_____ _____   _____ _____

Sum: _____   Sum: _____

3. Your cards: Partner's cards:

◯

_____ _____   _____ _____

Sum: _____   Sum: _____

4. Your cards: Partner's cards:

◯

_____ _____   _____ _____

Sum: _____   Sum: _____

5. Choose one round from above and explain how you determined which sum was greater.

Decimal Addition Problems (page 1 of 3)

Solve the problems below, showing your work clearly.

1. Nora takes three nuggets of gold to be weighed. One weighs 1.18 grams, another weighs 0.765 gram, and the third weighs 1.295 grams. What is the total weight of the gold?

2. On Monday Mercedes runs 2.25 miles, on Wednesday she runs 1.78 miles, and on Friday she runs 3.1 miles. How many total miles does she run?

3. On Tuesday Tavon runs 2.4 miles, on Thursday he runs 1.98 miles, and on Friday he runs 1.5 miles. How many total miles does he run?

4. Nora finds two more pieces of gold in her jewelry tray. One weighs 0.875 gram and the other one weighs 1.43 grams. What is the total weight of both pieces?

Decimal Addition Problems (page 2 of 3)

Solve the following problems, showing your work clearly.

5. 1.784 + 4.65 = _____

6. In the finals of the men's 100-meter butterfly at the 2004 Summer National Championships, the swimmers had these times for each 50 meters of the race.* Find the time it took them to swim the 100 meters.

Name	1st 50 Meters	2nd 50 Meters	Total
John Abercrombie	25.64	29.00	
Daniel Rohleder	25.18	28.99	
Matthew Scanlan	25.84	28.97	
Jonathan Schmidt	25.62	28.57	
William Stovall	25.48	28.76	

7. Place the swimmers in the order of their finish.

Place	Name	Time
1st		
2nd		
3rd		
4th		
5th		

*Source: www.usaswimming.org

Decimal Addition Problems (page 3 of 3)

Solve the following problems, showing your work clearly.

8. In the finals of the women's 100-meter butterfly at the 2004 Summer National Championships, the swimmers had these times for each 50 meters of the race.* Find the time it took them to swim the 100 meters.

Name	1st 50 Meters	2nd 50 Meters	Total
Kimberly Vandenberg	28.38	31.87	
Misty Hyman	27.89	32.46	
Morgan Scroggy	28.60	31.56	
Shelly Ripple Johnston	28.54	32.62	
Tanica Jamison	27.63	31.60	

9. Place the swimmers in the order of their finish.

Place	Name	Time
1st		
2nd		
3rd		
4th		
5th		

*Source: www.usaswimming.org

Gymnastics: Men's All-Around Scores

NOTE Students practice adding and ordering decimals to thousandths. Students should have thousandths grids available.

SMH **61–62, 63–65**

Here are some of the scores of six male gymnasts from the 2004 Olympics in Athens, Greece.

Name	Floor Exercise	Parallel Bars	Total Score
Rafael Martinez	9.500	9.700	
Dae Eun Kim	9.650	9.775	
Fabian Hambuechen	9.475	9.387	
Paul Hamm	9.725	9.837	
Marian Dragulescu	9.612	9.437	
Wei Yang	9.600	9.800	

1. Find each gymnast's total score for Floor Exercise plus Parallel Bars and record it on the chart.

2. Rank the gymnasts from the highest to the lowest score in Floor Exercise.

Ongoing Review

3. Which number is between 9.1 and 9.35?

   A. 9.020   **B.** 9.03   **C.** 9.200   **D.** 9.4

Close to 1

Find the sums for each pair of problems. Then circle the sum in each pair that is closer to 1.

> **NOTE** Students practice adding tenths, hundredths, and thousandths. Hundredths and thousandths grids should be available.
>
> **63–65**

1. 0.500 + 0.583 = _____   0.166 + 0.666 = _____

2. 0.725 + 0.333 = _____   0.166 + 0.5 + 0.333 = _____

3. 0.195 + 0.07 + 0.002 = _____   0.835 + 0.1 = _____

4. 0.7 + 0.301 = _____   0.48 + 0.06 = _____

5. 0.311 + 0.666 = _____   0.200 + 0.7 = _____

Adding Precipitation Amounts

The table below shows the average monthly precipitation for Juneau, Alaska.* Use the information on the table to solve each problem below, showing your work clearly. All amounts are recorded in inches.

NOTE Students practice adding decimals, using monthly precipitation amounts.

SMH 63–65

Jan.	Feb.	March	April	May	June	July	Aug.
4.54	3.75	3.28	2.77	3.42	3.15	4.16	5.32

1. How much precipitation did Juneau receive in January and February?

2. How much precipitation did Juneau receive in March and April?

3. How much precipitation did Juneau receive in May and June?

4. How much precipitation did Juneau receive in July and August?

5. How much precipitation did Juneau receive from January to August?

*Data are for the years 1961–1990.

Same Answer, Different Answer

Three of the four expressions in each set are equivalent. Without actually doing all the multiplication and division, circle the three equivalent expressions. Explain how you know that those three expressions are equivalent.

> **NOTE** Students use relationships among multiplication and division problems to find common products and quotients.
>
> SMH **33–34**

1. Which three expressions have the same product?

   2×40 420×4

   7×240 84×20

   How do you know?

2. Which three expressions have the same product?

   100×80 10×800

   1×800 $10 \times 10 \times 10 \times 8$

   How do you know?

3. Which three expressions have the same quotient?

   $720 \div 12$ $240 \div 4$

   $360 \div 6$ $600 \div 6$

   How do you know?

Ongoing Review

4. $568 \div 8 =$

   A. 710   **B.** 71   **C.** 70   **D.** 7.1

Speed Skating

Here are some of the results from the 2006 Torino Winter Olympics Men's Short-Track Speed Skating Competition. Determine each competitor's rank in the men's 1,500-meter race.

> **NOTE** Students solve real-world problems involving the math content of this unit.
>
> **58, 61–62**

Rank	Country	Skater's Name	Time (in minutes: seconds)
	CAN	Charles Hamelin	2:26.375
	HUN	Peter Darazs	2:24.969
	KOR	Ho-Suk Lee	2:25.600
	ITA	Fabio Carta	2:24.658
	USA	Apolo Anton Ohno	2:24.789
	CHN	JiaJun Li	2:26.005
	KOR	Hyun-Soo Ahn	2:25.341
	CAN	Mathieu Turcotte	2:24.558
	NED	Niels Kerstholt	2:24.962
	HUN	Viktor Knoch	2:26.806
	JPN	Satoru Terao	2:24.875

Explain your strategy for comparing the decimals.

Parrot Fire Kris Northern

"Rather than zoom into the fractal you can zoom into the edge of it and continually find the same pattern repeating itself much like the shoreline of a lake viewed from a plane." – **Kris Northern**

Investigations
IN NUMBER, DATA, AND SPACE®

Student Activity Book

How Many People? How Many Teams?   UNIT 7

How Many People?
How Many Teams?

Equivalence in Multiplication

Look at this equation:

$6 \times 9 = 3 \times 18$

1. Does doubling and halving always work? _____

2. Create a representation that shows your thinking.

Doubling and Halving

Ten dog walkers each walk 4 dogs. If half of the dog walkers do not show up for work, how many dogs do the rest of the dog walkers have to walk?

NOTE Students create equivalent expressions in multiplication and draw a representation to show that it is true.

SMH 33–34

1. Fill in this equation to match the story.

$10 \times 4 =$ _____

2. Create a representation to show that your equation is true.

Ongoing Review

3. What number makes this equation true?

$6 \times 8 = 3 \times$ _____

A. 4   **B.** 10   **C.** 16   **D.** 18

Tripling and Thirding

1. Fill in the missing numbers to make these equations true.

$2 \times 9 = 6 \times$ _____

$15 \times 4 = 5 \times$ _____

$7 \times 6 =$ _____ $\times 2$

2. Choose one of these equations and write a story problem about it.

3. Create a representation that shows the following:

When one number is tripled and the other number is divided by 3, the product is the same.

A Story About Tripling and Thirding

NOTE Students create a story and a representation for equivalent multiplication expressions.

SMH **33–34**

1. Make up a story problem to represent this equation:

   $3 \times 5 = 1 \times 15$

2. Create a representation to show that the equation is true.

Ongoing Review

3. What number makes this equation true?

   $8 \times 5 = \underline{\hspace{2cm}} \times 20$

   A. 4   **B.** 3   **C.** 2   **D.** 1

True or False?

Look at the equations below. Without finding the exact answer, determine whether each equation is true or false. Circle T or F.

NOTE Students are working on making equivalent multiplication expressions. They are looking for patterns and relationships in these equations that can help them determine whether the equations are true or false.

SMH 33–34

1. $3 \times 10 = 6 \times 5$ T or F

2. $10 \times 12 = 11 \times 11$ T or F

3. $20 \times 15 = 5 \times 30$ T or F

4. $6 \times 18 = 2 \times 36$ T or F

5. $4 \times 5 = 12 \times 10$ T or F

Fill in the blank to make each equation true.

6. $16 \times \underline{\hspace{2cm}} = 8 \times 8$

7. $2 \times 24 = 1 \times \underline{\hspace{2cm}}$

8. $1 \times 6 = 3 \times \underline{\hspace{2cm}}$

9. $6 \times 10 = 2 \times \underline{\hspace{2cm}}$

10. $5 \times 3 \times 2 = \underline{\hspace{2cm}} \times 2$

Finding Equivalent Expressions for 40 × 32 ✏️WRITING

1. Find as many different ways as you can to make this equation true.

    40 × 32 = _____ × _____

2. How are the numbers in your new expressions related to 40 × 32?

Name _____ Date _____

How Many People? How Many Teams? **Daily Practice**

Equivalent Multiplication Expressions

NOTE Students create equivalent multiplication expressions.

SMH 33–34

Fill in the blank to make each equation true.

1. $22 \times 6 = $ _____ $\times 12$

2. $12 \times 9 = 3 \times$ _____

3. $8 \times$ _____ $= 4 \times 16$

4. $4 \times 8 = 1 \times$ _____

5. $14 \times 6 = 42 \times$ _____

6. Make up four equations that contain equivalent multiplication expressions.

7. Choose one of your equations from Problem 6 and explain how you know that it is true.

Ongoing Review

8. $6 \times 64 = $ _____

   A. 70   **B.** 348   **C.** 364   **D.** 384

Equivalence in Multiplication

Find as many different ways as you can to make this equation true.

$$24 \times 18 = \underline{\hspace{2cm}} \times \underline{\hspace{2cm}}$$

NOTE Students make equivalent multiplication expressions. They look for patterns and relationships in these equivalent expressions.

SMH 33–34

Equivalence in Division

$$60 \div 10 = 120 \div \rule{2cm}{0.4pt}$$

1. Fill in the missing number to make the equation above true.

2. Write a story problem for the equation.

3. Make a sketch or diagram of your story.

4. Write more division expressions that fit this equation:

$$60 \div 10 = \rule{2cm}{0.4pt} \div \rule{2cm}{0.4pt}$$

Comparing Batting Averages

NOTE Students review comparing decimals.

SMH 61–62

Who had the better batting average?
Circle the higher batting average.

1. Ted Williams: 0.344 or Lou Gehrig: 0.340

2. Joe DiMaggio: 0.325 or Willie Mays: 0.302

3. Hank Aaron: 0.305 or Babe Ruth: 0.342

4. Rogers Hornsby: 0.358 or Ty Cobb: 0.366

5. Rod Carew: 0.328 or Stan Musial: 0.331

6. Reggie Jackson: 0.262 or Yogi Berra: 0.285

7. Johnny Bench: 0.267 or Mickey Mantle: 0.298

8. Jackie Robinson: 0.311 or Roberto Clemente: 0.317

Multiplication:
How Did I Solve It? (page 1 of 2)

Choose one or more of the following problems to solve.
(Solve additional problems on a separate sheet of paper.)

$75 \times 42 =$ $275 \times 8 =$ $186 \times 34 =$

$63 \times 24 =$ $134 \times 26 =$

1. Solve the problem in two ways. Use clear and concise
notation in your solution.

Problem: _____

First way:

Second way:

Multiplication:
How Did I Solve It? (page 2 of 2)

2. Write the problem you solved on page 13 and your
first steps. Your partner will use each of your first steps
to finish the problem.

Your partner's name: _____

Problem: _____

First step of first solution:

First step of second solution:

3. Compare solutions with your partner. How are
your solutions the same? How are they different?

Name   Date

How Many People? How Many Teams?   Daily Practice

Ordering Decimals

Place the decimals in order on the number line below.

NOTE Students practice placing decimals in order on a number line.

SMH 61–62

1. 1.9

2. 0.284

3. 1.899

4. 0.16

5. 0.235

6. 0.773

7. 0.821

8. 2.045

9. 0.492

10. 2.16

11. 2.492

12. 2.5

```
0      0.5      1      1.5      2      2.5
```

Multiplication Two Ways

NOTE Students show their flexibility and understanding of multiplication by solving problems in two ways.

SMH 30–32

Pick two of these problems to solve. Solve each problem two ways.

$95 \times 64 =$　　　$225 \times 25 =$

$187 \times 42 =$　　　$72 \times 45 =$

1. Problem: _____

First way:

Second way:

2. Problem: _____

First way:

Second way:

Multiplication Problems

Solve at least three of the multiplication problems below. Use clear and concise notation in your solution. (Solve additional problems on a separate sheet of paper.)

$78 \times 27 =$ $54 \times 41 =$ $743 \times 6 =$

$218 \times 15 =$ $145 \times 35 =$ $264 \times 24 =$

1. Problem: _____

2. Problem: _____

3. Problem: _____

Name _____ Date _____

How Many People? How Many Teams? Daily Practice

Finding Products 1

Solve the following problems. Show your work clearly.

NOTE Students solve multiplication problems and show their solutions.

SMH 30–32

1. $35 \times 92 =$ _____

2. $36 \times 118 =$ _____

Ongoing Review

3. $78 \times 25 =$ _____

    A. 9,500   **B.** 2,000   **C.** 1,950   **D.** 1,901

Solving 45 × 36

1. Solve this problem: 45 × 36 = _____

Your solution:

NOTE Students solve 45 × 36 and then ask someone else at home to solve it. The other person may use the strategy taught in school or may use an alternative method developed to solve multiplication problems easily.

 SMH 30–32

2. Ask an older person to solve the same problem and to record their strategy.

Their solution:

Two Algorithms: What Do They Mean? (page 1 of 2)

In both algorithms recorded below, the same problem is solved by breaking the numbers apart by place. With your partner, look closely at the solutions and make sense of what the notation shows.

Solution 1

$$\begin{array}{r} 142 \\ \times\ \ \ 36 \\ \hline 3{,}000 \\ 1{,}200 \\ 60 \\ 600 \\ 240 \\ +\ \ \ 12 \\ \hline 5{,}112 \end{array}$$

Solution 2

$$\begin{array}{r} 1 \\ 2\,1 \\ 142 \\ \times\ \ \ 36 \\ \hline 852 \\ +4{,}260 \\ \hline 5{,}112 \end{array}$$

Use each algorithm to record the solution to 138×24.

Solution 1

$$\begin{array}{r} 138 \\ \times\ 24 \\ \hline \end{array}$$

Solution 2

$$\begin{array}{r} 138 \\ \times\ 24 \\ \hline \end{array}$$

Two Algorithms:
What Do They Mean? (page 2 of 2)

Talk about these questions with your partner. Write your answers.

1. How would you explain to someone else what the numbers in each solution show? What do the small 1s and the small 2 in Solution 2 mean?

2. How are these two notations different from each other? How are they the same?

3. Challenge: Use both algorithms to show the solution to 184×61.

Name _____ Date _____

How Many People? How Many Teams?   Daily Practice

Finding Products 2

Solve the following problems. Show your work clearly.

NOTE Students solve multiplication problems and show their solutions.

SMH 30–32

1. $225 \times 32 =$ _____

2. $97 \times 63 =$ _____

Ongoing Review

3. $103 \times 26 =$ _____

A. 2,500   **B.** 2,678   **C.** 2,978   **D.** 26,780

Teams

Solve the problems below. Use clear and concise notation in your answers.

NOTE Students solve multiplication problems involving teams.

SMH **30–32**

1. There are 64 teams in a basketball tournament. Each team has 14 players. How many basketball players are in the tournament in all?

2. There are 135 teams in a soccer tournament. Each team has 32 players. How many soccer players are in the tournament in all?

3. There are 85 teams in a local softball league. Each team has 24 players. How many softball players are in the league in all?

Solving Multiplication Problems

Solve each problem below in two ways. One of the ways should be breaking the numbers apart by place, using one of the methods from page 21 (showing partial products).

First way: Second way:

1. $89 \times 42 =$

2. $97 \times 36 =$

3. $105 \times 72 =$

4. $248 \times 40 =$

5. $378 \times 69 =$

Name _____ Date _____

How Many People? How Many Teams?   Daily Practice

Measuring Distance

Solve the problems below, showing your work so that anyone looking at it would know how you solved the problem.

NOTE Students solve story problems involving addition of decimals.

SMH 63–65

1. On Monday, Margaret rollerbladed 4.55 miles. She rollerbladed 2.84 miles on Wednesday and 5.175 miles on Friday. What is the total number of miles she rollerbladed?

2. Renaldo ran 3.2 miles on Tuesday, 2.87 miles on Thursday, and 3.15 miles on Friday. What is the total number of miles he ran?

3. Terrence is preparing for a race. On Monday he bicycled 8.35 miles, and on Wednesday he bicycled 9.65 miles. What is the total number of miles he bicycled?

4. 0.69 mile + 0.041 mile + 2.03 miles = _____ miles

Name _____   Date _____

How Many People? How Many Teams?   Daily Practice

Squeeze Between

NOTE Students practice ordering decimals.

SMH 61–62

Fit one of the decimals shown on the cards between the pair of decimals in each exercise. Two cards will be left over.

1. 0.6 _____ 0.7

2. 0.25 _____ 0.15

3. 0.425 _____ 0.475

4. 0.075 _____ 0.125

5. 0.55 _____ 0.5

6. 0.675 _____ 0.725

7. 0.275 _____ 0.225

8. 0.025 _____ 0.075

9. 0.715 _____ 0.8

10. 0.4 _____ 0.3

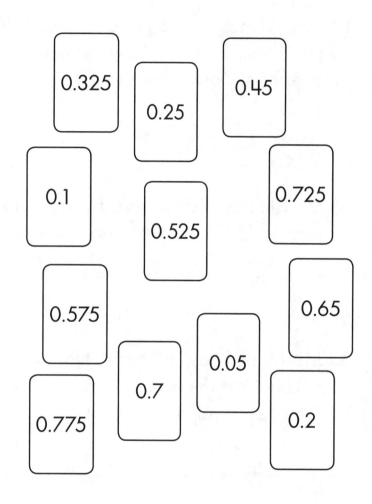

Ongoing Review

11. Which fraction is between 0 and $\frac{1}{2}$?

   A. $\frac{3}{2}$ **B.** $\frac{6}{8}$ **C.** $\frac{4}{6}$ **D.** $\frac{3}{8}$

Multiplication and Division Practice

Solve the following problems.

NOTE Students practice multiplication and division. They should remember that using the given story context can help them keep track of what they have solved and what they still need to solve.

SMH 30–32, 38–39

1. Mrs. Gomez has 56 packs of pencils. Each pack has 18 pencils. How many pencils does Mrs. Gomez have in all?

2. Mr. Chi has 340 markers. He wants to put them in bags of 24. How many bags does he need?

3. Ms. Marian has 285 books that she is going to donate to charity. If she puts 16 in a box, how many boxes will she need for all of her books?

4. Ms. Anderson has 123 boxes of books. Each box has 12 books in it. How many books does Ms. Anderson have in all?

Division Practice

Solve the following problems. Use clear and concise notation in your solutions.

1. $860 \div 64 = $ _____

2. There are 774 students at school. They will be placed in teams of 24 for a fundraiser. How many teams will there be?

3. $32\overline{)1{,}750}$

4. Georgia has 1,200 baseball cards that she wants to keep in envelopes. If she puts 26 cards in each envelope, how many envelopes does she need?

Sharing Equally

Share the supplies equally among the students in each class.

> **NOTE** Students use number sense to solve division problems. In these questions, the number of items left over does not matter.

Students in Ellen's class: 24
Stickers on each roll: 80

1. The class has 1 roll. Each student gets _____ stickers.

2. The class has 2 rolls. Each student gets _____ stickers.

3. The class has 5 rolls. Each student gets _____ stickers.

Students in Ami's class: 32
Counting cubes in each bucket: 120

4. The class has 1 bucket. Each student gets _____ cubes.

5. The class has 2 buckets. Each student gets _____ cubes.

6. The class has 5 buckets. Each student gets _____ cubes.

Students in Matteo's class: 22
Pens in each box: 240

7. The class has 1 box. Each student gets _____ pens.

8. The class has 2 boxes. Each student gets _____ pens.

9. The class has 5 boxes. Each student gets _____ pens.

Ongoing Review

10. Violet gave the clerk $5 for a $3.62 bag of grapes. How much change did she get back?

    A. $18.10   **B.** $8.62   **C.** $2.38   **D.** $1.38

Dividing by Multiples of 10

Try to solve all the following problems mentally. If you do not solve a problem mentally, show how you solved it.

> **NOTE** Students practice dividing numbers that are multiples of 10.

1. $120 \div 20 =$

2. $\dfrac{90}{30}$

3. $500 \div 50 =$

4. $90\overline{)720}$

5. $4{,}900 \div 70 =$

6. $3{,}000 \div 60 =$

7. $3{,}200 \div 80 =$

8. $450 \div 30 =$

9. $4{,}800 \div 20 =$

10. $5{,}600 \div 80 =$

Counting Around the Room

Solve the following problems. Use clear and concise notation in your solutions.

1. The school marching band is counting around the room by 11s. Each person says only one number. The first student says 11, and the last student says 737. How many students counted?

2. The school Math Club counts by a certain number. Each person says only one number. The last student says 910. If there are 35 students in the Math Club by what number are they counting?

3. Mr. Smith's class is counting by 75s, and students can count more than once. The first person says 75, and the last person says 4,050. How many 75s do the students count?

4. There are 32 students in Ms. Chen's class. They count by a certain number, and the last student says 1,280. If each person says only one number, by what number are they counting?

Name   Date

How Many People? How Many Teams?   **Daily Practice**

Dividing 500 by 16

Find the quotient and remainder for Problem 1.
Use your answer to solve the other problems.

NOTE Students interpret remainders
in division situations.

SMH 37

1. 500 ÷ 16 is _____ with a remainder
   of _____.

2. Vicky needs 500 paper plates. There are 16 plates in
   a bag. How many bags should she buy? _____

3. Sean has 500 pounds of apples for 16 horses. How
   many pounds can each horse have? _____

4. Ed has 500 tomato plants. He is putting 16 plants in
   each box. How many boxes can he fill? _____

5. Sharon is shipping 500 wind-up toy cows. She will
   put 16 or 17 cows in a box. Describe the shipment
   of cows.

   _____ boxes with 16 cows and _____ boxes
   with 17 cows

Ongoing Review

6. Which set of multiples are shaded in
   the table?

   A. multiples of 3

   B. multiples of 4

   C. multiples of 5

   D. multiples of 6

2	4	6	8
3	6	9	12
4	8	12	16
5	10	15	20

© Pearson Education 5

Classroom Counting Puzzles

Solve these problems. Use clear and concise notation in your solutions.

NOTE Students continue to practice solving multiplication and division problems.

SMH 14

1. Ms. Green's class has 29 students and counts by 45s. Each person says only one number. If the first person says 45, what does the last person say?

2. Mr. Black's class counts by 25s. Each person says only one number. The first person says 25, and the last person says 700. How many students are in Mr. Black's class?

3. Mr. Blue's class has 31 students. They count by a certain number, and the last person says 899. If each person says only one number, by what number are they counting?

4. Ms. Yellow's class has 28 students. They count by 65s, and each person says only one number. If the first student says 65, what does the last student say?

Division Starter Problems (page 1 of 3)

For Problems 1–6, choose a starter problem (first step), "a" or "b," to complete each problem. If you would like to use a different starter problem from the two listed, write it on the blank labeled "c." Then, use the starter problem you have chosen to solve the final problem.

1. $2,000 \div 42 =$

   a. Start by solving $840 \div 42$.

   b. Start by solving 40×42.

   c. _____

2. Renaldo has 650 marbles. He wants to put them in bags that hold 28 marbles each. How many full bags of marbles will he have?

   a. Start by solving $560 \div 28$.

   b. Start by solving 28×10.

   c. _____

Division Starter Problems (page 2 of 3)

3. 30)‾2,554‾

   a. Start by solving 30 × 80.

   b. Start by solving 1,200 ÷ 30.

   c. _____

4. Tomas made 825 cookies for a bake sale. He puts them in 22 boxes. If each box has the same numbers of cookies, how many cookies are in each box? How many cookies are left over?

   a. Start by solving 22 × 30.

   b. Start by solving 440 ÷ 22.

   c. _____

© Pearson Education **5**

Division Starter Problems (page 3 of 3)

5. $499 \div 2$

   a. Start by solving 2×200.

   b. Start by solving $500 \div 2$.

   c. _____

6. There are 1,080 students at Packer Elementary School. They are organized in 40 equal-sized groups for a field trip. How many students are in each group?

   a. Start by solving $800 \div 40$.

   b. Start by solving 25×40.

   c. _____

Classroom Supplies (page 1 of 2)

Use the information below to answer the following
questions. Record your work on a separate sheet of paper.

Item	Unit	Cost
Pencils	12 per package	$0.99
Pens	12 per package	$1.98
Erasers	10 per package	$1.29
Glue sticks	18 per package	$3.49

Grade	Number of Students
Third	80
Fourth	100
Fifth	150

1. The third-grade teachers want to purchase 3 pencils for each student.

How many packages of pencils do they need to buy?

What is the total cost?

2. The third-grade teachers want to purchase 1 glue stick for each student.

How many packages of glue sticks do they need to buy?

What is the total cost?

3. The fourth-grade teachers want to purchase 2 erasers for each student.

How many packages of erasers do they need to buy?

What is the total cost?

4. The fourth-grade teachers want to buy 2 pencils and 1 glue stick for each student.

How many packages of pencils do they need to buy? Of glue sticks?

What is the total cost?

© Pearson Education 5

Classroom Supplies (page 2 of 2)

5. The fifth-grade teachers want to buy 2 pencils and 2 pens for each student.

How many packages of pencils do the teachers need to buy?

Of pens?

What is the total cost?

6. A local business gave the fifth-grade teachers $50.00 for classroom supplies. Whatever money the teachers do not spend, they have to return, so they want to spend as much as possible on supplies.

What items could the teachers buy?

How many of each item would each student get?

What is the total cost?

How much money do the teachers have to return?

Finish It Up!

You are given the first step for solving each problem. Use this step to find the solution. Show your work on another sheet of paper.

NOTE Students solve multiplication and division problems, using a given first step.

SMH 30–32, 38–39

1. Find 401 × 13 by first solving 400 × 10.

   401 × 13 = _____

2. Find 74 × 23 by first solving 2 × 74.

   74 × 23 = _____

3. Find 8 × 643 by first solving 8 × 600.

   8 × 643 = _____

4. Find 342 ÷ 5 by first solving 300 ÷ 50.

   342 ÷ 5 = _____

5. Find 871 ÷ 16 by first solving 16 × 50.

   871 ÷ 16 = _____

Ongoing Review

6. Each square on the grid shows 1 square block. What is the shortest distance from the square to the triangle?

   A. 3 blocks   **C.** 4 blocks

   B. 5 blocks   **D.** 7 blocks

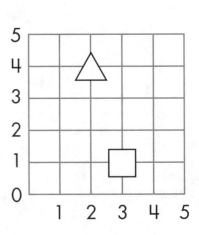

Counting Puzzles

Solve these problems. Use clear and concise notation in your solutions.

NOTE Students solve division problems.

SMH **38–39**

1. Ms. Jones's class has 26 students and they count by the same number. Each student says only one number. The last student to count says 1,040. By what number are they counting?

2. Mr. Smith's class counts by 75s. Each student says only one number. The last student to count says 2,025. How many students counted?

3. Ms. Plant's room counts by 42s. Each student says only one number. The first student says 42, and the last student says 1,218. How many students counted?

Name _____   Date _____

How Many People? How Many Teams?   **Daily Practice**

Different First Steps

Write two different first steps that you could use to solve each problem. Choose one of your first steps and find the solution. Show your work on another sheet of paper.

> **NOTE** Students show two different first steps for the same problem.
>
> **SMH** 30–32, 38–39

1. To find 73×29, I could start with _____ or _____.

The answer is _____.

2. To find $87 \div 15$, I could start with _____ or _____.

The answer is _____.

3. To find $578 \div 4$, I could start with _____ or _____.

The answer is _____.

4. To find 482×7, I could start with _____ or _____.

The answer is _____.

5. To find $318 \div 26$, I could start with _____ or _____.

The answer is _____.

Ongoing Review

6. Which plant height measurements would make this graph?

A. 1, 3, 5, 8, 8   **C.** 1, 3, 3, 5, 7

B. 1, 1, 1, 4, 4   **D.** 1, 5, 6, 6, 8

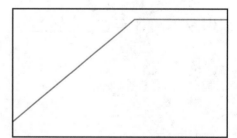

Multiplying Money

Solve each problem.

NOTE Students multiply amounts of money that are close to the next dollar.

SMH 30–32

1. $9.99
     ×   12
     ___

2. $7.98 × 5 = _____

3. $14.97 × 6 = _____

4. $29.99
     ×   6
     ___

5. $34.99 × 3 = _____

Division:
How Did I Solve It? (page 1 of 2)

Choose one or more of the following problems to solve.
(Solve additional problems on a separate sheet of paper.)

$498 \div 9 =$ $\qquad$ $376 \div 6 =$ $\qquad$ $685 \div 34 =$

$2,837 \div 52 =$ $\qquad$ $3,989 \div 49 =$

1. Solve the problem in two ways. Use clear and concise notation in your solution.

   Problem: _____

   First way:

   Second way:

How Many People? How Many Teams?

Division:
How Did I Solve It? (page 2 of 2)

2. Write the problem you solved on page 47 and the
2 first steps you used to solve it. Your partner will use
each of your first steps to finish the problem.

Your partner's name: _____

Problem: _____

First step of first solution:

First step of second solution:

3. Compare solutions with your partner. How are
your solutions the same? How are they different?

Name _____   Date _____

How Many People? How Many Teams?   **Daily Practice**

Making Estimates

> **NOTE** Students use multiples of 10, familiar combinations, and doubling strategies to make estimates for more difficult multiplication and division problems.

Estimate the products.

1. Problem: 34×62

$30 \times 62 =$ _____

2. Problem: $843 \div 8$

$840 \div 8 =$ _____

3. Problem: 79×61

$80 \times 61 =$ _____

4. Problem: $2,764 \div 7$

$2,800 \div 7 =$ _____

5. Problem: 29×58

$30 \times 60 =$ _____

6. Problem: $719 \div 19$

$720 \div 20 =$ _____

7. Problem: 32×418

$32 \times 400 =$ _____

8. Problem: $463 \div 82$

$480 \div 80 =$ _____

9. Problem: 673×76

$700 \times 80 =$ _____

10. Problem: $3,128 \div 64$

$3,000 \div 60 =$ _____

Ongoing Review

11. What does this shape look like after a right turn of 90 degrees?

A. 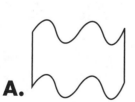   **B.**    **C.** 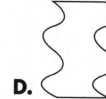   **D.**

Division Practice

Solve each problem. Use clear and concise notation.

NOTE Students solve division problems.

SMH 38–39

1. $514 \div 8 =$ _____

2. $559 \div 28 =$ _____

3. $874 \div 21 =$ _____

4. $691 \div 33 =$ _____

Division Two Ways

Solve each problem two ways.
Show each solution clearly.

NOTE Students solve division problems in two different ways.

SMH 38–39

1. 768 ÷ 32 = _____

First way:

Second way:

2. 968 ÷ 48 = _____

First way:

Second way:

Ongoing Review

3. Which number is not a factor of 3,000?

A. 35 **B.** 50 **C.** 100 **D.** 150

Field Day: Third to Fifth Grades

Use the information on the charts below to solve the
problems on pages 53 and 57–60.

Note: Teams compete against their own grade level, unless otherwise stated.

Intermediate Grades at Hancock Elementary School

Third Grade

Teacher	Number of Students
Mr. Willis	22
Mrs. Alvarez	21
Ms. Manning	19
Ms. Garcia	21

Fourth Grade

Teacher	Number of Students
Ms. Voight	28
Ms. Wilkos	30
Mrs. Chong	29
Mr. Anderson	28

Fifth Grade

Teacher	Number of Students
Mrs. Yan	30
Mr. Clark	32
Ms. Dwyer	31
Mrs. Brennan	28
Mrs. Driver	29

Field Day Refreshments

The Hancock PTA wants to purchase at least one nutrition bar and at least one drink for each student for the Third to Fifth Grade Field Day. They have budgeted $200 for these refreshments.

The table shows the cost of items, which cannot be purchased individually. Also, refer to the information given on page 52.

Item	Cost
Nutrition Bar	$3.99 for box of 24
Fruit Juice (8 oz)	$3.29 for box of 12
Bottled Water (8 oz)	$4.99 for case of 36

1. What should the PTA order? How many boxes or cases of each item will the PTA need to order?

2. Find the total cost of the order.
   Show your work below.

Large and Small Hunt

In each row, circle the largest product or quotient. Then underline the smallest.

NOTE Students use various strategies for solving multiplication and division problems.

SMH **30–32, 38–39**

1. 46×77 or 67×51 or 39×86

2. $1{,}120 \div 14$ or $1{,}680 \div 24$ or $3{,}400 \div 34$

Ongoing Review

3. What might this data show?

A. the heights of first graders

B. the heights of houses

C. the heights of basketball players

D. the heights of dogs

Individual	Inches
A	78
B	84
C	80
D	75
E	82
F	84

How Many People? How Many Teams?

Multiplication and Division Practice

Try to solve all of the following problems mentally. If you do not solve a problem mentally, show how you solved it.

NOTE Students practice multiplication and division using multiples of 10 or 100. Students should try to solve these problems mentally.

1. $5 \times 800 = $ _____

2. $\begin{array}{r} 70 \\ \times\ 6 \\ \hline \end{array}$

3. $375 \times 10 = $ _____

4. $13 \times 15 = $ _____

5. $15 \times 40 = $ _____

6. $540 \div 9 = $ _____

7. $240 \div 8 = $ _____

8. $420 \div 6 = $ _____

9. $850 \div 17 = $ _____

10. $420 \div 3 = $ _____

Field Day Activities: Relay Race

Teams of 8 students compete in the relay race. How many teams are in each grade? If there are extra students, write how many students are not on teams.

Refer to the information given on page 52. Complete the chart below. Use the space under the chart to show your work.

Grade	Number of Teams	Students Not on a Team
Third		
Fourth		
Fifth		

Field Day Activities: Kickball

There will be 11 teams at each grade level for the kickball games. This time, everyone needs to be on a team.

Refer to the information given on page 52. Complete the chart below. Use the space under the chart to show your work.

Grade	Number of Students on a Team
Third	
Fourth	
Fifth	

Field Day Activities: Tug of War

The final activity will be a gigantic tug of war. All of the fourth graders will be on one side. All of the fifth graders will be on the other side. The third graders will be split up so that the two sides have an equal number of students.

Refer to the information given on page 52. Answer the following questions. Show your work below.

1. How many third graders will be with fourth graders? _____

2. How many third graders will be with fifth graders? _____

3. What will be the total number of students on each team? _____

Field Day Lunch and Cleanup

Refer to the information given on page 52. Use the total number of students in Grades 3, 4, and 5 to answer the following questions. Show your solutions clearly.

1. At lunchtime, students are placed in groups of 30 and sent to classrooms to eat. How many classrooms have 30 students? How many students are in the classroom that is not full?

2. At the end of the day, all of the students are placed on 28 teams to clean the school and playground. How many students are on each team?

Name _____ Date _____

How Many People? How Many Teams?   Daily Practice

Two-Part Problems

Each problem has two parts. You'll need the first answer to solve the second problem.

> **NOTE** Students use multiplication and division to solve word problem situations, some of which have remainders.
>
> **SMH** 30–32, 38–39

1. **PART 1** Suppose that there are 48 balloons in a bag. If you buy 10 bags, how many balloons will you have? _____

PART 2 There are 37 people coming to your party. How many balloons can each person have? _____

2. **PART 1** A factory made 1,800 yellow duck buttons. They put four on each card. How many cards were filled? _____

PART 2 The factory put 24 cards in each box. How many boxes were filled? _____

3. **PART 1** You and 8 friends wash 57 cars. Suppose that you charge $12 per car. How much money will you earn? _____

PART 2 If you share what you earn with your 8 friends, how much money will each person get? _____

Ongoing Review

4. Which fraction is equivalent to $\frac{1}{2}$?

A. $\frac{1}{4}$ **B.** $\frac{2}{8}$ **C.** $\frac{4}{16}$ **D.** $\frac{4}{8}$

5. Which fraction is equivalent to $\frac{3}{4}$?

A. $\frac{6}{6}$ **B.** $\frac{6}{8}$ **C.** $\frac{6}{12}$ **D.** $\frac{3}{9}$

More Multiplication and Division Practice

NOTE Students practice multiplication and division using multiples of 10 or 100. Students should try to solve these problems mentally.

Try to solve all of the following problems mentally. If you do not solve a problem mentally, show how you solved it.

1. $100 \times 23 =$ _____

2. $25 \times 700 =$ _____

3. $3 \times 400 =$ _____

4. 150
$\underline{\times\ 8}$

5. $1{,}600 \times 5 =$ _____

6. $1{,}800 \div 900 =$ _____

7. $2{,}600 \div 13 =$ _____

8. $3{,}500 \div 70 =$ _____

9. $25\overline{)900}$

10. $6{,}000 \div 12 =$ _____

Field Day Problems

Solve each problem. Show your work.

1. For the water balloon toss, the PTA needs to buy 8 bags of balloons. Each bag has 175 balloons in it and costs $2.49.

How many individual balloons does the PTA need to buy? _____

How much will the PTA spend on balloons? _____

2. The PTA needs to buy 50 batons for the relay races. Batons can be ordered in packages of 6. Each package costs $4.99.

How many packages of batons does the PTA need to order? _____

How much will the PTA spend on batons? _____

3. The Hancock PTA needs to order 348 participation ribbons for Field Day. These ribbons cost $2.89 for a package of 20.

How many packages does the PTA need to order? _____

How much will the PTA spend on ribbons? _____

Multiplying and Dividing Large Numbers (page 1 of 2)

Solve the following problems. Use clear and concise notation in your solutions.

1.   748
      $\times$ 64

2. $657 \times 93 =$ _____

3. $2{,}401 \times 27 =$ _____

4. Write a story problem that represents one of the multiplication problems above.

Multiplying and Dividing Large Numbers (page 2 of 2) ✏️WRITING

5. 7,899 ÷ 84 = _____

6. 75)‾4,856

7. 10,000 ÷ 68 = _____

8. Write a story problem that represents one of the division problems above.

Name _____ Date _____

How Many People? How Many Teams?   **Daily Practice**

Multiplying and Daily Practice
Dividing Large Numbers

NOTE Students solve multiplication and division problems with large numbers and show their solutions.

SMH **30–32, 38–39**

1. $1,522 \times 21 =$ _____

2. $8,425 \div 25 =$ _____

3. $2,734 \times 35 =$ _____

Ongoing Review

4. Which division equation is related to $126 \times 18 = 2,268$?

A. $2,268 \div 18 = 126$ **C.** $126 \div 2,268 = 18$

B. $126 \div 18 = 2,268$ **D.** $126 \div 6 = 21$

Juice and Oranges

Solve each problem below. Use clear and concise notation to show your solution.

> **NOTE** Students solve related problems in a story context. Students should use an answer they have already found to help them solve the related problem.
>
> **SMH** 30–32

1. A store orders 75 cases of juice. Each case holds 24 cans of juice. How many cans of juice will be delivered?

2. The next week, the store orders 125 cases of juice. How many cans of juice will be delivered this time?

3. The same store orders 80 cases of oranges. Each case holds 18 oranges. How many oranges will be delivered?

4. The next week, the store orders 150 cases of oranges. How many oranges will be delivered this time?

Name   Date

How Many People? How Many Teams?   Daily Practice

Multiplication and Division Two Ways

NOTE Students solve multiplication and division problems with large numbers in two different ways.

SMH **30–32, 38–39**

Solve the following problems in two ways.
Show each solution clearly.

1. $267 \times 48 =$ _____

First way:

Second way:

2. $7,302 \div 51 =$ _____

First way:

Second way:

Ongoing Review

3. $646 \times 52 =$ _____

A. 305,293   **B.** 35,921   **C.** 33,592   **D.** 5,529

Milk Cartons

Solve each problem below. Use clear
and concise notation to show your solution.

One case of milk contains 48 cartons.

NOTE Students solve related
problems in a story context.
Students should try to use an
answer they have already found to
help them solve the next problem.

SMH 38–39

1. If there are 960 cartons of milk in the
cafeteria, how many cases of milk are there?

2. If there are 1,920 cartons of milk in the cafeteria,
how many cases of milk are there?

3. If there are 2,880 cartons of milk in the cafeteria,
how many cases of milk are there?

Name _____ Date _____

How Many People? How Many Teams?   Daily Practice

Supersonic Flight

Solve the following problems. Show your
work on another sheet of paper.

NOTE Students practice
multiplication in the context
of a story problem.

SMH 30–32, 38–39

A plane that travels at Mach 1 is traveling at the
speed of sound. Mach 2 is twice the speed of sound,
Mach 3 is three times the speed of sound, and so on.
(The speed of a jumbo passenger jet is less than Mach 1.)

1. In the table below, find the missing speeds
in miles per hour (mph).

2. If a plane travels at Mach 5,
how far does it travel per *minute*? _____

Mach Speeds*	
Mach 1	680 mph
Mach 2	1,360 mph
Mach 3	
Mach 4	
Mach 5	

*based on a speed of sound of
680 mph in the stratosphere

The X-43, an unmanned scramjet plane, can
reach a speed of nearly Mach 10. An aircraft
flying at Mach 10 could travel between
Los Angeles, CA and Rome, Italy in under
two hours!

3. a. Find the speed in miles per hour of the X-43. _____
b. How far does the X-43 travel per *minute*? _____

Parrot Fire Kris Northern

"Rather than zoom into the fractal you can zoom into the edge of it and continually find the same pattern repeating itself much like the shoreline of a lake viewed from a plane." – **Kris Northern**

Investigations
IN NUMBER, DATA, AND SPACE®

Growth Patterns

Growth Patterns

Growth Stories: Tara and Nat (page 1 of 2)

Read the following growth stories of Tara and Nat and complete the table and graph. You may choose to start with either the graph or the table.

Tara's Story

Tara was 80 centimeters when she was 2 years old.
She grew at a steady rate until she was 10 years old.

Nat's Story

Nat was 85 centimeters tall when he was 2 years old.
Nat grew quickly until he was 4 years old. Then he
grew at a slower, steady rate.

Age (years)	Tara's Height (cm)	Nat's Height (cm)
2		
3		
4		
5		
6		
7		
8		
9		
10		

Growth Stories: Tara and Nat (page 2 of 2)

Tara and Nat

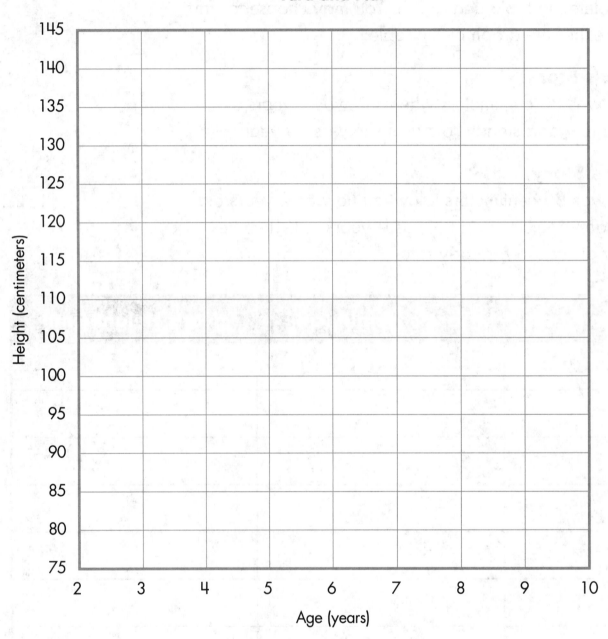

Height (centimeters) / Age (years)

How Far to 10,000?

Imagine you are traveling along a number line that goes from 0 to 10,000.

NOTE Students use addition and subtraction to solve problems.

SMH 8–9, 10–13

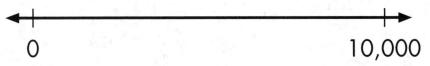

0   10,000

Solve the following problems and explain how you found the distance between the numbers.

1. How far is it from 5,725 to 10,000?

2. How far is it from 19 to 10,000?

3. How far is it from 8,107 to 10,000?

4. How far is it from 291 to 10,000?

Ongoing Review

5. 6,004 + _____ = 10,000

   A. 3,960   **C.** 4,060

   B. 3,996   **D.** 4,996

Solving Subtraction Problems

Solve each problem below. Use clear and concise notation to show how you solved each problem.

NOTE Students practice solving subtraction problems.

SMH **10–13**

1.   13,240
    – 4,317

2. $18,647 - 9,782 =$ _____

3. $10,000 - 2,152 =$ _____

4.   9,007
   –6,241

Representing Growth Stories: Tony, Maya, and Susie (page 1 of 3)

Read the following growth stories of Tony, Maya, and Susie, and fill in the table on page 6. Then, sketch a graph on page 7 of these three students' growth from age 2 to age 10. When you are satisfied with your sketch, make a final draft. Use a different color for each student. Make a key to show which color is for which student.

1. Tony's Story

Tony was 85 centimeters tall on his second birthday. He grew at a steady rate until he was 10 years old. On his tenth birthday, he was 135 centimeters tall.

2. Maya's Story

Maya was 90 centimeters tall on her second birthday. She grew quickly until she was 7 years old. Then she grew very slowly until she was 10 years old. On her tenth birthday, she was 145 centimeters tall.

3. Susie's Story

Susie was 80 centimeters when she was 2 years old. She grew at a steady rate until she was 6 years old. Between ages 6 and 8, Susie grew more quickly. On her eighth birthday she was 115 centimeters tall. Then she grew more slowly until she was 10 years old. On her tenth birthday, she was 120 centimeters tall.

Growth Patterns

Representing Growth Stories:
Tony, Maya, and Susie (page 2 of 3)

Age (years)	Tony's Height (cm)	Maya's Height (cm)	Susie's Height (cm)
2			
3			
4			
5			
6			
7			
8			
9			
10			

Growth Patterns

Representing Growth Stories:
Tony, Maya, and Susie (page 3 of 3)

Tony, Maya, and Susie

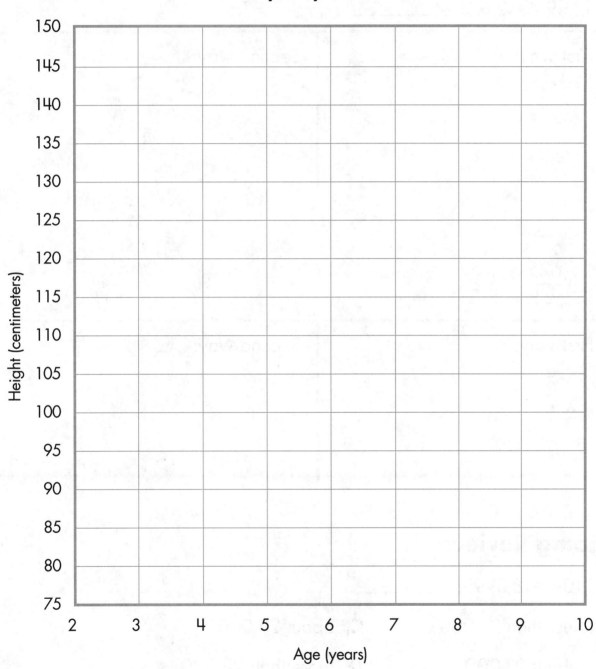

Daily Practice

Solve Two Ways, Addition

Solve each problem in two ways. Use clear
and concise notation in your solutions.

> **NOTE** Students practice
> flexibility in solving
> addition problems.
>
> **SMH** 8–9

1.   13,495 + 2,623 = _____

First way:	Second way:

2.   7,625
     +4,378

First way:	Second way:

Ongoing Review

3. 15,109 + 8,099 is _____.

    A. less than 23,000   **C.** about 24,000

    B. about 23,000   **D.** more than 24,000

Flickerbill's Growth (page 1 of 3)

The Flickerbill is 4 centimeters tall at birth. It grows
3 centimeters each year. Finish the table for the
Flickerbill's growth.

Age (years)	Height (cm)
0 (birth)	4
1	7
2	10
3	
4	
5	
6	
7	
8	
9	
10	
15	
100	

© Pearson Education **5**

Flickerbill's Growth (page 2 of 3)

Answer the following questions about the Flickerbill's growth.

1. How did you find the Flickerbill's height for age 15?

2. How did you find the Flickerbill's height for age 100?

Flickerbill's Growth (page 3 of 3)

Complete the graph for the Flickerbill's growth up to age 10.

Graph of Flickerbill's Growth

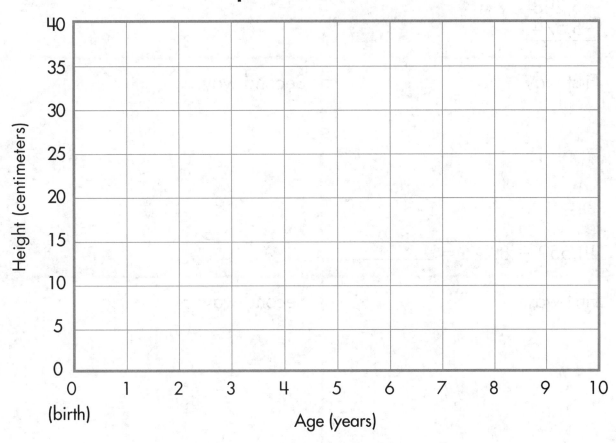

Solve Two Ways, Subtraction

Solve each problem in two ways. Use clear and concise notation in your solutions.

> **NOTE** Students practice flexibility in solving subtraction problems.
>
> **SMH** 10–13

1. $\begin{array}{r} 6{,}248 \\ -5{,}574 \\ \hline \end{array}$

First way: Second way:

2. $14{,}559 - 8{,}276 = $ _____

First way: Second way:

Ongoing Review

3. Which of the following is **true**?

   A. $10{,}890 + 5{,}012 < 7{,}200 + 6{,}848$

   B. $13{,}992 + 2{,}004 < 17{,}073 - 7{,}106$

   C. $16{,}010 - 8{,}449 > 12{,}107 - 5{,}991$

   D. $4{,}160 + 9{,}040 > 7{,}150 + 7{,}217$

Growth Patterns

Ricardo's and Myriam's Growth Graphs (page 1 of 2)

NOTE Students practice using line graphs to analyze data.

SMH **69**

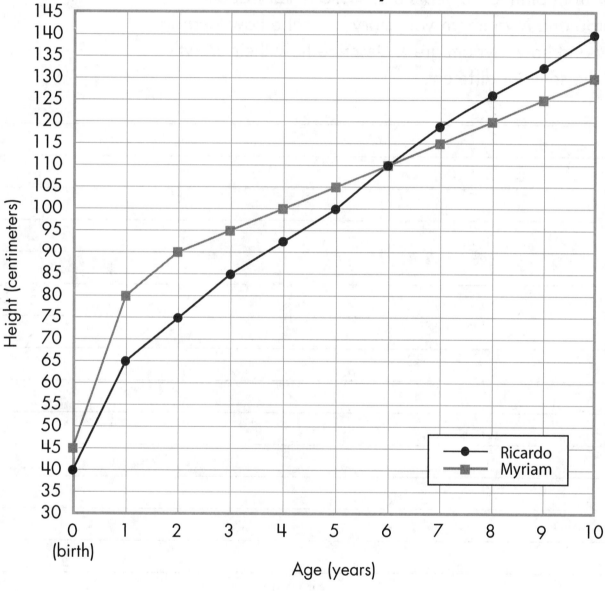

Ricardo and Myriam

Height (centimeters)

Age (years)

Ricardo
Myriam

Ricardo's and Myriam's Growth Graphs (page 2 of 2)

The graphs on page 13 show how Ricardo and Myriam grew from birth to 10 years old. Write a story about Ricardo and Myriam. In your story, describe how Ricardo grew and how Myriam grew. Describe how their growth was the same or different.

_____

_____

_____

_____

_____

_____

_____

_____

_____

_____

_____

_____

_____

_____

_____

_____

_____

_____

_____

_____

_____

Growth Patterns

The Krink, the Trifoot, and the Water Weasel (page 1 of 2)

Each of these three animals from Rhomaar grows the same amount each year. Finish the table.

Age (years)	Height (cm)		
	Krink	**Trifoot**	**Water Weasel**
0 (birth)	1	15	15
1	6	17	20
2	11	19	25
3	16	21	30
4			
5			
6			
7			
8			
9			
10			
15			
100			

The Krink, the Trifoot, and the Water Weasel (page 2 of 2)

Using the values from the table on page 15, make a graph for the heights of each of the three animals from birth to age 10.

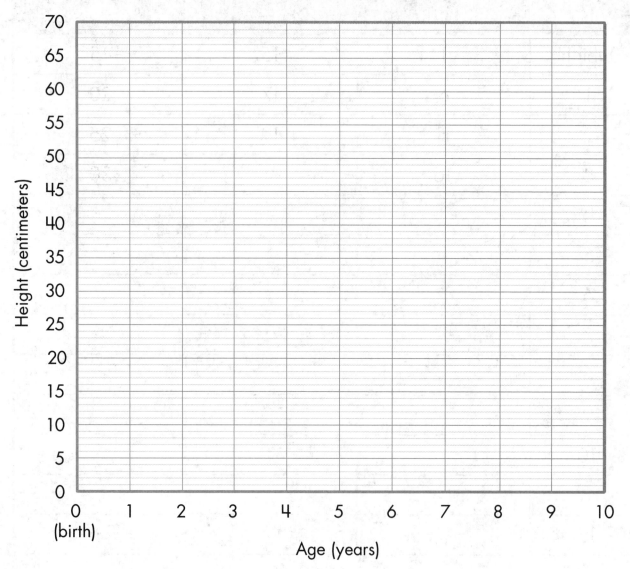

Animals of Rhomaar

Related Problems

Solve the related problems in each set below.
As you work on these problems, think about
how solving the first problem in each set may
help you solve the others.

---

1. 9,474 − 400 = _____

9,474 − 500 = _____

9,474 − 550 = _____

2. 5,160 + 435 = _____

5,160 + 445 = _____

5,160 + 455 = _____

---

3. 14,698 + 3,000 = _____

14,698 + 3,200 = _____

14,698 + 3,202 = _____

4. 21,738 + 300 = _____

21,738 + 4,300 = _____

21,738 + 4,305 = _____

---

5. 6,000 − 1,020 = _____

5,900 − 1,020 = _____

5,910 − 1,020 = _____

6. 42,536 − 20,000 = _____

42,536 − 18,000 = _____

42,536 − 18,200 = _____

Fastwalker (page 1 of 3)

The Fastwalker grows by a special rule. It is different from the other animals the scientists have studied on Rhomaar so far. See whether you can figure out the pattern. Fill in the rest of the table for the Fastwalker's growth.

Age (years)	Height (cm)
0 (birth)	1
1	2
2	4
3	7
4	11
5	16
6	
7	
8	
9	
10	

Fastwalker (page 2 of 3)

Using the values from the table on page 18, make a graph showing the Fastwalker's growth.

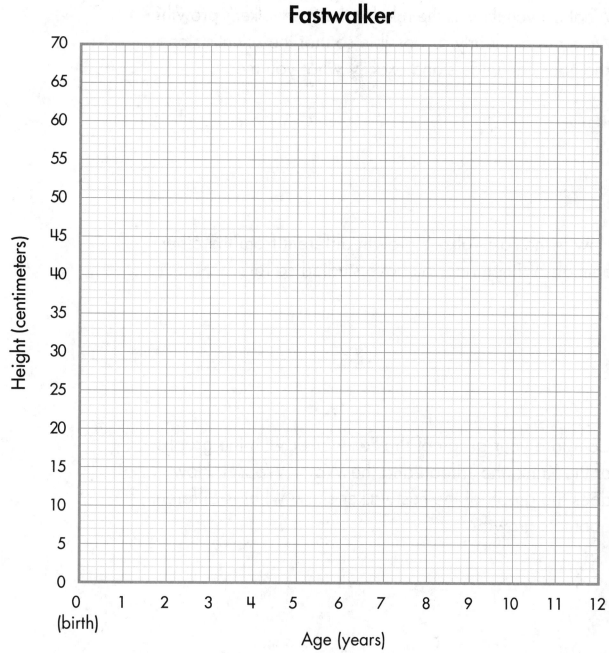

Fastwalker

Fastwalker (page 3 of 3) ✏️

Look at your table and graph for the Fastwalker.
Use them to answer these questions.

1. What do you think is the rule for the Fastwalker's growth?
   Write this as clearly as possible so that the scientists on
   Rhomaar can understand exactly what you mean.

2. How is the Fastwalker's growth different from the other
   animals of Rhomaar you have studied so far?

3. Compare your graph of the Fastwalker with the graphs
   of the Krink, the Trifoot, and the Water Weasel. How
   does the graph of the Fastwalker show what is different
   about its growth?

Addition Problems

Solve each problem below. Use clear and concise notation to show how you solved each problem.

NOTE Students practice solving addition problems.

SMH 8–9

1. $42.45
        + 17.68

2. 7,598 + 8,264 = _____

3. 25,222 + 5,194 = _____

4.   33,180
        +25,872

Ongoing Review

5. Which number is seven thousand more than 44,771?

   A. 52,771   **B.** 51,771   **C.** 50,771   **D.** 45,471

Spiraltail's and Inksnake's Growth Table

NOTE Students record data in a table.

SMH 66–67, 70–71

The Spiraltail and the Inksnake grow the same amount each year. Finish the growth table for the Spiraltail and the Inksnake.

Age (years)	Height (cm)	
	Spiraltail	**Inksnake**
0 (birth)	2.5	15
1	5	16.5
2	7.5	18
3	10	19.5
4		
5		
6		
7		
8		
9		
10		

3 Tiles Across:
Total Number of Tiles (page 1 of 2)

Here is a row of
3 square tiles.

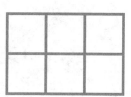

Now make another row of 3 tiles.
It takes 6 tiles to make 2 rows.

1. Continue adding rows of 3 tiles.
Complete this table.

Number of Rows	Total Number of Tiles
1	3
2	6
3	
4	
5	
6	
10	
15	
20	
100	
n	

Growth Patterns

3 Tiles Across:
Total Number of Tiles (page 2 of 2)

2. How did you find the number of tiles for 100 rows?

3. Write a rule or formula to find the total number
of tiles for any number of rows.

3 Tiles Across: Perimeter (page 1 of 2)

Here is a row of 3 square tiles. The tiles are
1 centimeter by 1 centimeter squares. The perimeter
of the rectangle they make is 8 centimeters.

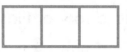

Make a rectangle with 2 rows of 3 tiles.
What is the perimeter of this rectangle?

1. Continue adding rows of tiles. Find the perimeter
   of each rectangle. Fill in the table below.

Number of Rows	Perimeter (cm)	Arithmetic Expression
1	8	
2		
3		
4		
5		
6		
10		
15		
20		
100		
n		

3 Tiles Across: Perimeter (page 2 of 2)

2. How does the perimeter change every time you add a row of tiles?

3. How did you find the perimeter for 100 rows?

4. Write a rule or formula to find the perimeter for any number of rows.

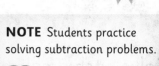

Subtraction Problems

Solve each problem below. Use clear and concise notation to show how you solved each problem.

> **NOTE** Students practice solving subtraction problems.
>
> **SMH** 10–13

1. 100,000
   − 1,327

2. 31,413 − 8,772 = _____

3. 12,495 − 3,637 = _____

4. $845.59
   − 82.76

Ongoing Review

5. The fifth graders at Lake Elementary collected 91,070 pennies for charity. Their goal was to collect 100,000 pennies. How many more pennies do they need to reach their goal?

   A. 8,930   **B.** 9,030   **C.** 9,130   **D.** 9,930

More Addition Problems

NOTE Students practice solving addition problems.

SMH 8–9

Solve each problem below. Use clear and concise notation to show how you solved each problem.

1. $37{,}090 + 15{,}662 =$

2. $\begin{array}{r} 40{,}009 \\ +21{,}993 \\ \hline \end{array}$

3. $\begin{array}{r} 29{,}989 \\ +15{,}114 \\ \hline \end{array}$

4. $\begin{array}{r} 52{,}006 \\ +\ 8{,}985 \\ \hline \end{array}$

Concert Time

The Composites are playing a sold-out concert at the Gopherdome, which holds 40,000 people. The concert starts at 8:00 P.M. Answer the questions below and show your work clearly.

NOTE Students practice solving addition and subtraction problems in story contexts.

 SMH 8–9, 10–13

1. At 7:00 pm., 24,725 people are at the concert. How many people have not arrived yet?

2. a. By 7:30 pm., 9,590 more people have arrived. How many people are at the concert now?

b. How many people have not arrived yet?

3. By 8:00 pm., 38,638 people are at the concert. How many people have not arrived?

Name _____ Date _____

_____ Tiles Across:
Total Number of Tiles (page 1 of 3)

Make a row of tiles with the number assigned to your
group. Add on rows until you have a clear idea about how
the number of tiles increases.

1. Complete this table.

Number of Rows	Total Number of Tiles	Arithmetic Expression
1		
2		
3		
4		
5		
6		
10		
15		
20		
100		
n		

_____ Tiles Across:
Total Number of Tiles (page 2 of 3)

2. How does the total number of tiles change every time you add a row?

3. How did you find the number of tiles for 100 rows?

4. Write a rule or formula to find the total number of tiles for any number of rows.

_____ Tiles Across: Total Number of Tiles (page 3 of 3)

5. Make a graph for _____ Tiles Across: Total Number of Tiles

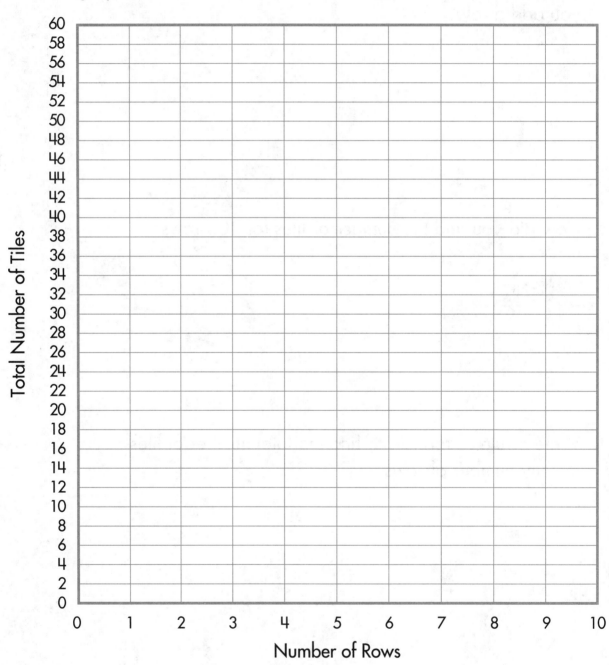

6. What do you notice about the graph? Write your observations on a separate sheet of paper.

Date

Tiles Across:
Perimeter (page 1 of 3)

Make a row of tiles with the number assigned to your group. Add on rows until you have a clear idea about how the perimeter increases.

1. Complete this table.

Number of Rows	Perimeter (cm)	Arithmetic Expression
1		
2		
3		
4		
5		
6		
10		
15		
20		
100		
n		

_____ Tiles Across:
Perimeter (page 2 of 3)

2. How does the perimeter change every time you add a row?

3. How did you find the perimeter for 100 rows?

4. Write a rule or formula to find the perimeter for any number of rows.

Growth Patterns

_____ Tiles Across:
Perimeter (page 3 of 3)

5. Make a graph for _____ Tiles Across: Perimeter

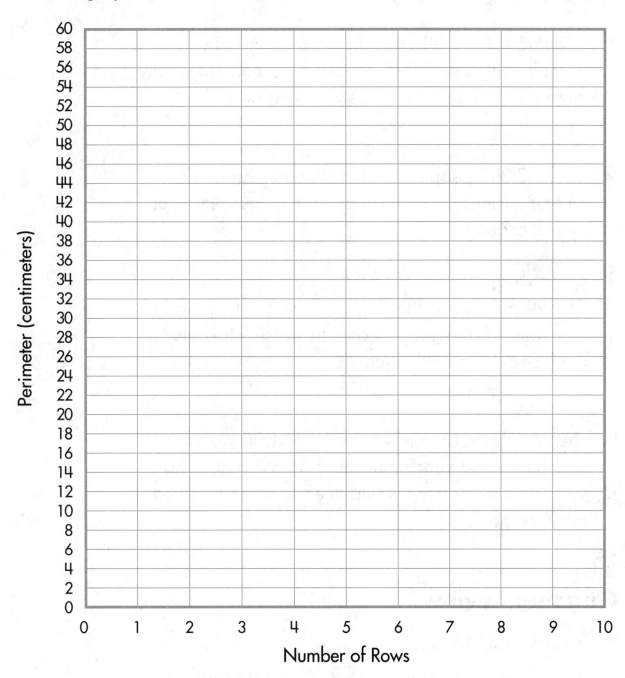

Number of Rows

6. What do you notice about the graph? Write your observations on a separate sheet of paper.

Parade

Solve each of the following problems. Show your work clearly. Be sure to answer the question posed by the story.

NOTE Students practice solving problems in story contexts using addition and/or subtraction.

SMH 8–9, 10–13

1. In a large city, 2,842 people marched in this year's parade. Last year, 3,237 people marched. How many more people marched in last year's parade?

2. Of the 2,842 people who marched this year, 1,276 were musicians. How many other marchers were not musicians?

3. 56,394 people lined the streets to watch the parade. Last year, 47,826 people came to watch. How many more people came this year?

4. The parade organizers would like 65,000 people to come to next year's parade. If 56,394 came this year, how many more would need to come next year to meet the goal?

Ongoing Review

5. 34,079 + 8,001 is _____.

   A. more than 43,000

   B. about 43,000

   C. about 42,000

   D. less than 42,000

More Subtraction Problems

Solve each problem below. Use clear and concise
notation to show how you solved each problem.

NOTE Students
practice solving
subtraction problems.

 SMH 10–13

1.   53,000
       −19,815

2.   60,500
       − 9,750

3. 71,050 − 69,185 =

4. 48,771 − 15,964 =

Growth Patterns

10 Tiles Across:
Total Number of Tiles (page 1 of 3)

Make a row of 10 tiles in your group. Add rows until you
have a clear idea about how the number of tiles increases.

1. Complete this table.

Number of Rows	Total Number of Tiles	Arithmetic Expression
1		
2		
3		
4		
5		
6		
10		
15		
20		
100		
n		

10 Tiles Across:
Total Number of Tiles (page 2 of 3)

2. How does the total number of tiles change every time you add a row?

3. How did you find the number of tiles for 100 rows?

4. Write a rule or formula to find the total number of tiles for any number of rows.

10 Tiles Across:
Total Number of Tiles (page 3 of 3)

5. Make a graph for 10 Tiles Across: Total Number of Tiles.

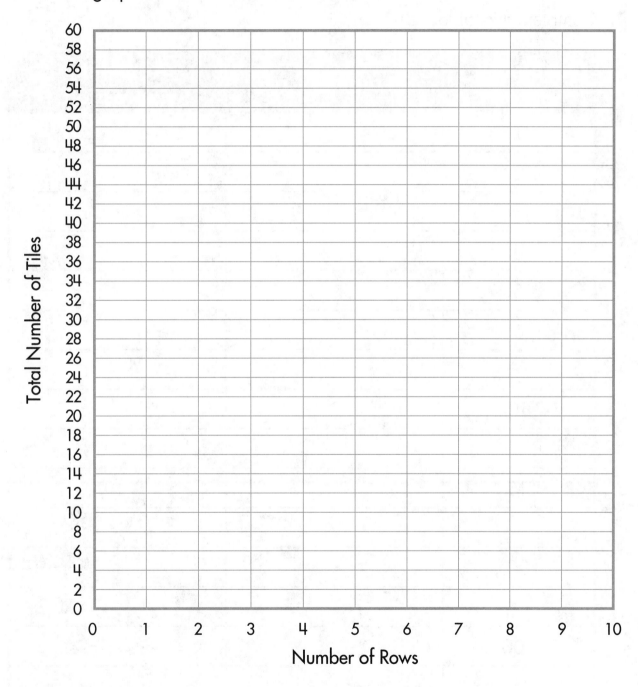

6. What do you notice about the graph? Write your observations on a separate sheet of paper.

10 Tiles Across: Perimeter (page 1 of 3)

Make a row of 10 tiles with your group. Add on rows until
you have a clear idea about how the perimeter increases.

1. Complete this table.

Number of Rows	Perimeter (cm)	Arithmetic Expression
1		
2		
3		
4		
5		
6		
10		
15		
20		
100		
n		

10 Tiles Across: Perimeter (page 2 of 3)

2. How does the perimeter change every time you add a row?

3. How did you find the perimeter for 100 rows?

4. Write a rule or formula to find the perimeter for any number of rows.

10 Tiles Across: Perimeter (page 3 of 3)

5. Make a graph for 10 Tiles Across: Perimeter.

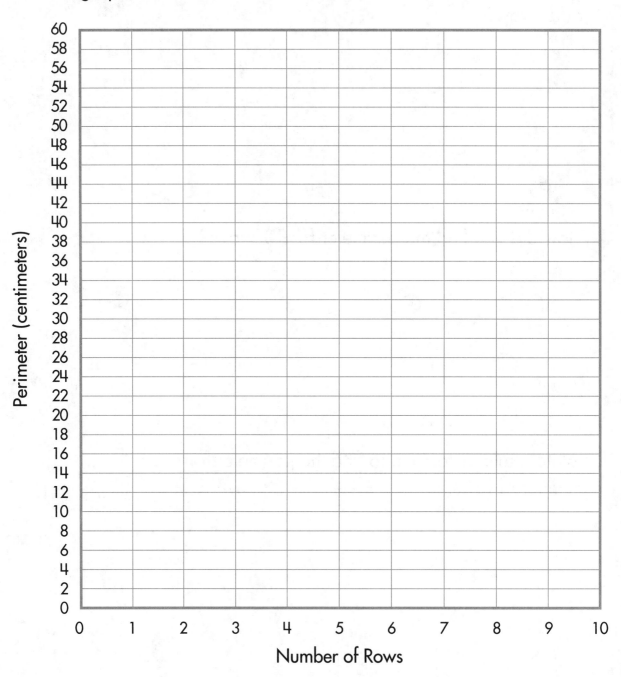

6. What do you notice about the graph? Write your observations on a separate sheet of paper.

Growth Patterns

Shopping

Solve each of the following problems. Show your work clearly. Be sure to answer the question posed by the story.

NOTE Students practice solving addition and subtraction problems in story contexts.

SMH **8–9, 10–13**

1. Renaldo went to the store and bought items that cost $23.59, $12.47, and $15.68. How much money did he spend all together?

2. Olivia also went shopping and spent a total of $61.78. She bought 3 items. She spent $24.79 on one item and $33.34 on another item. What was the cost of the third item?

3. Walter went shopping, and his total purchases were $73.34. He paid with a $100 bill. How much change did he receive?

4. Write and solve your own story problem using these numbers: $14.58 + $27.17 + $29.85 = _____

Ongoing Review

5. The sum of $46.95 and $34.06 is _____.

   A. about $70.00   **C.** about $80.00

   B. about $75.00   **D.** about $85.00

How Far to 75,000?

NOTE Students find the difference between the given number and 75,000.

SMH 10–13

For each problem below, find out how far it is from the given number to 75,000 on the 100,000 chart. For problems 4 and 5, choose the number you want to start with and write it in the blank.

1. Start at 2,006. How far to 75,000? _____

2. Start at 28,031. How far to 75,000? _____

3. Start at 46,608. How far to 75,000? _____

4. Start at _____. How far to 75,000? _____

5. Start at _____. How far to 75,000? _____

Adding 2 Penny Jar (page 1 of 3)

Imagine that a Penny Jar contains 2 pennies.
For each round, 2 more pennies are added.

1. Complete this table.

Round	Total Number of Pennies	Arithmetic Expression
Start with	2	
1		
2		
3		
4		
5		
6		
10		
15		
20		
100		
n		

Adding 2 Penny Jar (page 2 of 3)

2. How does the total number of pennies change
in each round?

3. How did you find the total number of pennies for
100 rounds?

4. Write a rule or formula to find the total number
of pennies for any number of rounds. Explain why
this works.

Adding 2 Penny Jar (page 3 of 3)

5. Make a graph for this Penny Jar.

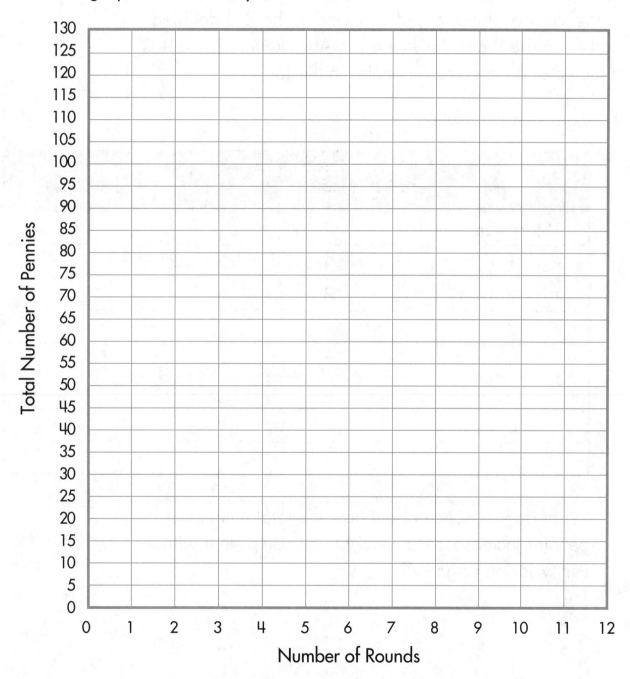

6. What do you notice about the graph? Write your observations on a separate sheet of paper.

Growth Patterns

The Doubling Penny Jar (page 1 of 2)

Now, imagine a different kind of Penny Jar. It starts with 2 pennies inside. For each round, the number of pennies in the jar is doubled. So, after Round 1, the 2 is doubled and there are 4 pennies in the jar. After Round 2, the 4 is doubled and there are 8 pennies in the jar.

1. Complete this table.

Number of Rounds	Total Number of Pennies	Arithmetic Expression
Start with	2	
1	4	
2	8	
3		
4		
5		
6		
7		

2. What do you notice about how the total number of pennies increases? How would you compare it with the Penny Jar on page 47?

The Doubling Penny Jar (page 2 of 2)

3. Make a graph for the Doubling Penny Jar.

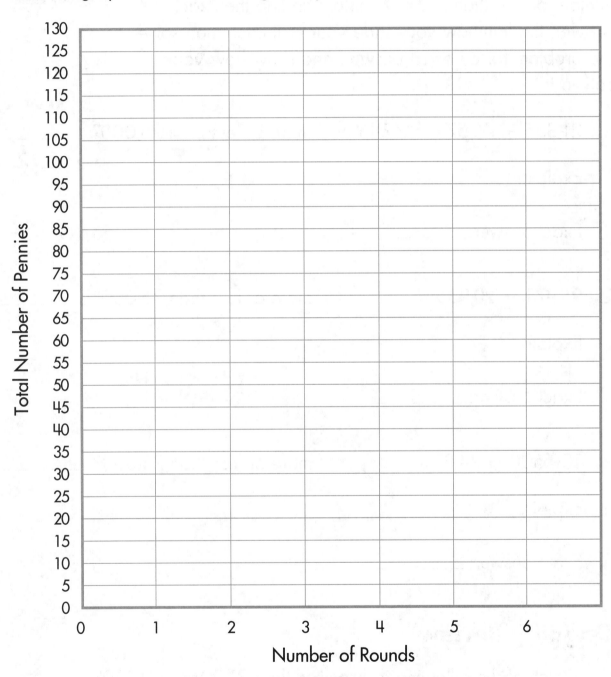

4. What do you notice about the graph? How does it compare to the graph for the Penny Jar on page 49? Write your observations on a separate sheet of paper.

More or Less Than 75,000?

For each problem below, estimate whether the answer is more or less than 75,000 without finding the exact answer. Explain how you made your estimate. Then solve the problem for an exact answer, and show how you solved it.

> **NOTE** Students estimate the sums of addition problems.

1. 21,355 + 45,572 + 7,745   more or less than 75,000? _____

   Explain.

   Exact answer: _____

2. 95,471 − 20,435   more or less than 75,000? _____

   Explain.

   Exact answer: _____

3. 100,500 − 24,800   more or less than 75,000? _____

   Explain.

   Exact answer: _____

Ongoing Review

4. Which of the following is **greater** than 91,006 − 71,130?

   A. 36,211 − 18,400   **C.** 66,117 − 49,003

   B. 25,000 − 9,907   **D.** 49,902 − 28,884

Growing Squares (page 1 of 2)

Start with a 1 × 1 square. Add tiles
until the figure is a 2 × 2 square.

Then add tiles until it is a 3 × 3 square. Figure out
the number of tiles you need as the square grows.

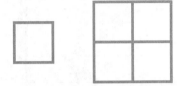

1. Complete this table.

Length of One Side of the Square (cm)	Number of Tiles	Arithmetic Expression
1		
2		
3		
4		
5		
6		
10		
15		
20		

2. What do you notice about how the number
of tiles increases? Write your observations on a
separate sheet of paper.

Growing Squares (page 2 of 2)

3. Make a graph for Growing Squares.

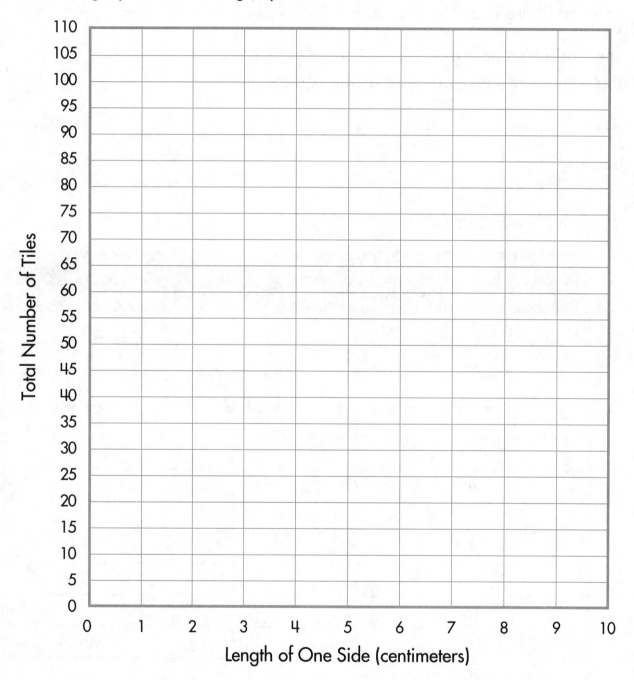

4. What do you notice about the graph? Write your observations on a separate sheet of paper.

Solving Addition Problems

NOTE Students practice solving addition problems.

SMH 8–9

Solve each problem below. Use clear and concise notation to show how you solved each problem.

1.   24,199
     +61,431

2. 18,264 + 39,247 = _____

3. 3,155 + 21,052 = _____

4.   19,050
     +39,241

Ongoing Review

5. Which number is closest to 28,835?

A. 28,800   **B.** 28,900   **C.** 28,090   **D.** 29,000

Admission Price

Fun Times Amusement Park is a popular destination. In the chart below are the admission prices to the park.

Categories	Price
Adults	$53.75
Teens (12–17 years)	$49.25
Children (2–11 years)	$45.35
Infants (under 2 years)	Free

Solve each problem below. Use clear and concise notation to show how you solved each problem.

1. What is the total admission price for 2 adults and 1 child?

2. What is the total admission price for 1 adult and 3 teens?

3. What is the total admission price for 1 adult, 2 teens, and 2 children?

4. What is the total admission price for 4 adults, 1 teen, and 1 child?

5. Is $150 enough for 2 adults and 1 teen's admission to the park? _____

Growth Patterns

Staircase Towers: Jumps of 1 (page 1 of 3)

Start with a 1 × 1 square. Add tiles to make a staircase
with jumps of 1 each time, like this:

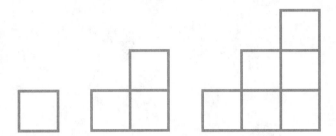

1. Complete this table for Staircase Towers: Jumps of 1.

Length of the Bottom Edge (cm)	Number of Tiles	Arithmetic Expression
1	1	
2	3	
3	6	
4		
5		
6		
7		
8		
9		
10		

Staircase Towers: Jumps of 1 (page 2 of 3)

2. What patterns do you see in the table?

3. What do you think the graph will look like? Why?

Staircase Towers: Jumps of 1 (page 3 of 3)

4. Make a graph for Staircase Towers: Jumps of 1.

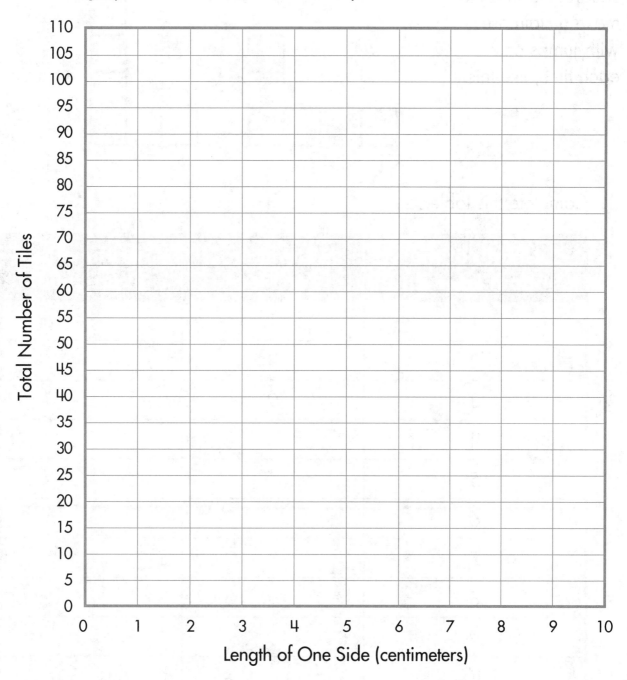

5. What do you notice about the graph? Write your
observations on a separate sheet of paper.

Growth Patterns

Staircase Towers: Jumps of 2 (page 1 of 3)

Start with a 1 × 1
square. Add tiles to
make a staircase
with jumps of 2
each time, like this:

1. Complete this table.

Length of the Bottom Edge (cm)	Number of Tiles	Arithmetic Expression
1	1	
2	4	
3	9	
4		
5		
6		
7		
8		
9		
10		

Growth Patterns

Staircase Towers: Jumps of 2 (page 2 of 3)

2. What patterns do you see in the table?

3. What do you think the graph will look like? Why?

Staircase Towers: Jumps of 2 (page 3 of 3)

4. Make a graph for Staircase Towers: Jumps of 2.

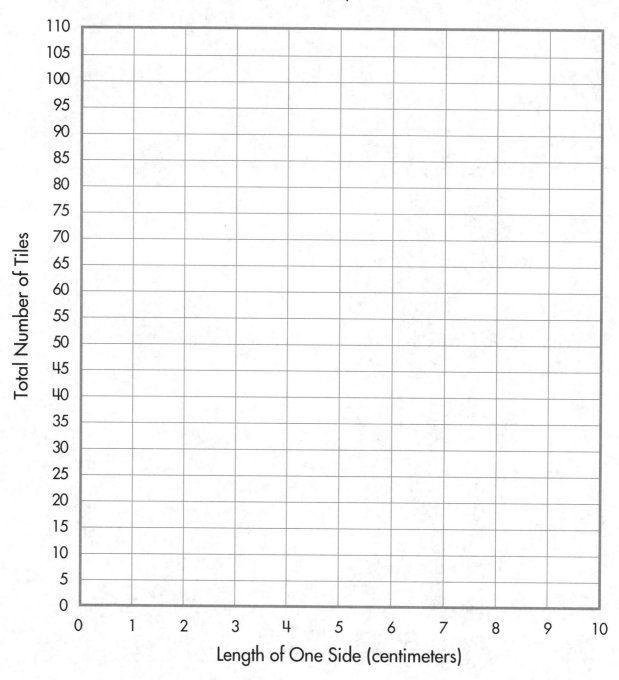

5. What do you notice about the graph? Write your observations on a separate sheet of paper.

Amusement Park Attendance

NOTE Students practice solving addition and subtraction problems.

SMH 8–9, 10–13

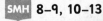

Fun Times Amusement Park is a popular destination. In the chart below is the number of people who visited the park during a busy Memorial Day weekend.

Days	Number of People
Saturday	45,464
Sunday	31,295
Monday	23,091

Solve each problem below. Use clear and concise notation to show how you solved each problem.

1. How many people visited Fun Times Amusement Park during Memorial Day weekend?

2. How many more people visited the park on Saturday than on Monday?

3. During Labor Day weekend, 75,306 people attended Fun Times Amusement Park. How many more people visited during Memorial Day weekend than during Labor Day weekend?

Ongoing Review

4. Which is the closest estimate of 17,000 + 49,000 + 8,000?

   A. 70,000   **B.** 75,000   **C.** 80,000   **D.** 90,000

Helping Hands (page 1 of 2)

1. Vince, Marta, and Paula each wants to donate at least $30 to charity. Vince plans to donate $6 now plus $2 per week. Marta plans to donate $10 now plus $1 per week. Paula is not donating any money now, but she will donate $3 per week. Complete the table.

NOTE Students solve real-world problems involving the math content of this unit.

SMH 72–73

Week	Vince's Total Donation ($)	Marta's Total Donation ($)	Paula's Total Donation ($)
start	6	10	0
1	8	11	3
2			
3			
4			
5			
10			
15			
20			

Helping Hands (page 2 of 2)

2. Make a graph to show each person's donations.

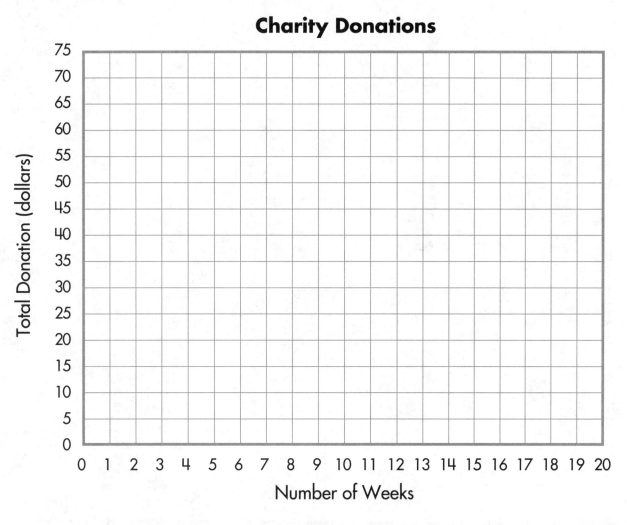

Charity Donations

a. Which person will be the first to donate a total
of $30?

b. How many weeks will it take Vince to reach the $30
goal? Marta? Paula?

c. If Vince, Marta, and Paula continue making
donations at the same rate, how much will each
person have donated after 1 year?

"Rather than zoom into the fractal you can zoom into the edge of it and continually find the same pattern repeating itself much like the shoreline of a lake viewed from a plane." – **Kris Northern**

Investigations
IN NUMBER, DATA, AND SPACE®

Student Activity Book

How Long Can You Stand on One Foot?   UNIT 9

How Long Can You Stand on One Foot?

Collecting Data on Balancing

Use the information below to collect data about classmates and balancing.

1. Let the person get comfortably balanced on one foot before closing his or her eyes.

2. Timing starts when the person closes his or her eyes and says "go."

3. The person can wiggle in place but cannot hop or spin. Some part of the foot the person is standing on must always touch the floor.

4. The foot that is up cannot touch anything (such as the floor, a wall, or a piece of furniture).

5. Four things can end the test:
   a. The person puts his or her foot down.
   b. The person opens his or her eyes.
   c. The person hops or touches an object for balance.
   d. The person balances for 3 minutes.

6. The person gets one practice trial for each foot.

7. If the person is still balancing at 3 minutes, stop the test and record 180 seconds (3 minutes) as the time. When you are collecting the data, be sure to have your eyes on the clock or watch before the person says "go."

Your Own Balancing Data (in seconds):

Left foot: _____   Right foot: _____

Absent Days

NOTE Students describe and summarize a set of data.

SMH 82

In December, the assistant principal posted the number of days students were absent from school during the last four months. The following bar graph represents the Grade 5 data.

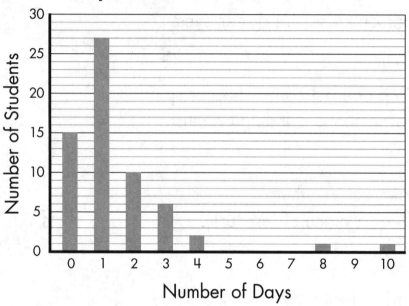

Days Absent from School — Grade 5

1. Describe at least two things you notice about the data.

2. What is the range of data in this graph?

Ongoing Review

3. How many students were absent 3 days?

A. 0   **B.** 3   **C.** 5   **D.** 6

Name _____ Date _____

How Long Can You Stand on One Foot?   Homework

How Long Do Adults Balance? (page 1 of 2)

> **NOTE** Students collect data on how long adults can balance on one foot. Then students will compare these data with data they already collected from their class. Help students collect data from two or more adults.

Collecting Data on Balancing

1. Let the person get comfortably balanced on one foot before closing his or her eyes.

2. Timing starts when the person closes his or her eyes and says "go."

3. The person can wiggle in place but not hop or spin. Some part of the foot the person is standing on must always touch the floor.

4. The foot that is up cannot touch anything (such as the floor, a wall, or a piece of furniture).

5. Four things can end the test:
   a. The person puts his or her foot down.
   b. The person opens his or her eyes.
   c. The person hops or touches an object for balance.
   d. The person balances for 3 minutes.

6. The person gets one practice trial for each foot.

7. If the person is still balancing at 3 minutes, stop the test and record 3 minutes as the time.

When you are collecting the data, be sure to have your eyes on the clock or watch before the person says "go."

How Long Do Adults Balance? (page 2 of 2)

How long can adults balance on each foot with their eyes closed? Test two or more adults, and record the results. Follow the same rules you used at school. The person can practice first, but only once, on each foot. Remember that 3 minutes is the longest time you can record.

Name of Adult	Balance Time on Right Foot (in seconds)	Balance Time on Left Foot (in seconds)

Do you think the group of adults will be different from or the same as you and your classmates? How might they be different or the same? Write two predictions.

1.

2.

Mystery Balancers Data

Mystery Balancers A

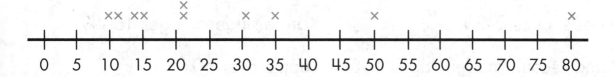

Mystery Balancers B

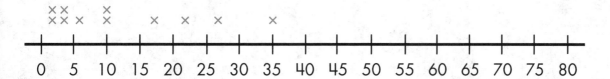

Mystery Balancers C

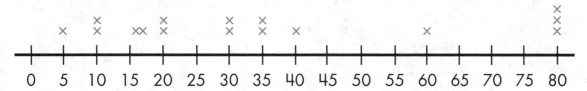

Mystery Balancers D

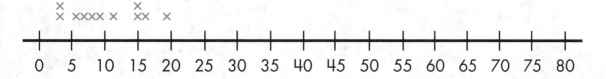

Who Are the Mystery Balancers?

The Mystery Groups

Gymnasts, ages 9–20   Karate students, ages 16–49

First and second graders, ages 6–8   People over 50

Who do you think the mystery balancers are? Explain
what evidence in the data makes you think so.

Set A:

Set B:

Set C:

Set D:

Solve Two Ways

Solve each problem two ways. Use clear and concise notation in your solutions.

> **NOTE** Students show their flexibility and understanding of multiplication by solving problems in two ways.
>
> **SMH** 30–32

1.　$148 \times 35 =$ _____

First way:	Second way:

2.　$\begin{array}{r} 268 \\ \times\ 43 \\ \hline \end{array}$

First way:	Second way:

Division Practice

Choose two of these problems to solve. Solve each problem two ways.

NOTE Students show their flexibility and understanding of division by solving problems in two ways.

SMH 38–39

$1,554 \div 75$ $79\overline{)3,164}$ $8,904 \div 21$ $6,478 \div 42$

1. Problem:

First way:	Second way:

2. Problem:

First way:	Second way:

How Long Can You Stand on One Foot?

Comparison Charts (page 1 of 2)

Comparison Chart of Adult and Student Data: Left Foot				
What are you comparing?	Adults	Students	Who is better?	Agree?

Comparison Charts (page 2 of 2)

Comparison Chart of Adult and Student Data: Right Foot				
What are you comparing?	Adults	Students	Who is better?	Agree?

Equivalent Problems

NOTE Students make equivalent multiplication and division problems and look for patterns and relationships in equations.

 SMH 33–34

1. Fill in the missing numbers to make these equations true.

$16 \times 16 =$ _____ $\times 32$

$24 \times 12 = 8 \times$ _____

$40 \times$ _____ $= 20 \times 18$

2. Find as many different ways as you can to make this equation true.

$48 \times 12 =$

3. Fill in the missing numbers to make these equations true.

$120 \div 4 = 240 \div$ _____ $144 \div 12 =$ _____ $\div 6$

4. Find as many different ways as you can to make this equation true.

$500 \div 50 =$

Conclusions About Balancing Data ✏️ WRITING

1. Given your comparisons of the data for students balancing on one foot and adults balancing on one foot, who would you say is better at balancing on one foot, adults or fifth-grade students?

   _____

   Why do you think so? Include evidence from the data.

2. Why do you think it might be that fifth-grade students or adults are better at balancing on one foot?

3. What other experiments could you do to learn more about this topic?

Comparing Data

Study the two data sets. Then complete the statements.

NOTE Students compare two sets of data.

SMH 85–88

Joshua's Class: Balancing Time in Seconds (Left Foot)

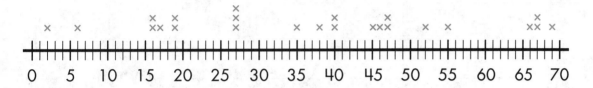

Talisha's Class: Balancing Time in Seconds (Left Foot)

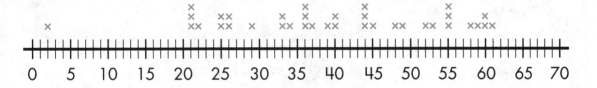

1. Half of Joshua's class balanced for more than _____ seconds.

2. Half of Talisha's class balanced for more than _____ seconds.

3. On another sheet of paper, write which class balances better. Give reasons for your opinion.

Ongoing Review

4. Ben wants to graph these numbers: 26, 30, 28, 28, 30, 27.
   Which line plot should he use?

   A. 0   1   2   3   4

   B. 26   27   28

   C. 26   27   28   29

   D. 26   28   30   32   34

How Long Have Fifth Graders Lived in Their Homes? (page 1 of 2)

NOTE Students compare two sets of data that are represented in bar graphs.

SMH 85–88

Students in fifth grade at the Bartley School in Pineville and students in fifth grade at School #3 in Maple City were asked the following question: How long have you lived in the home you live in now?

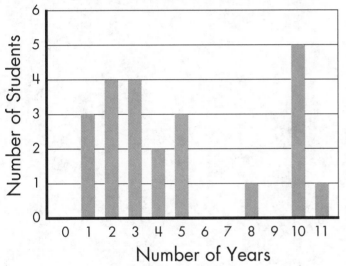

Amount of Time Fifth Graders at the Bartley School Have Lived in Their Homes

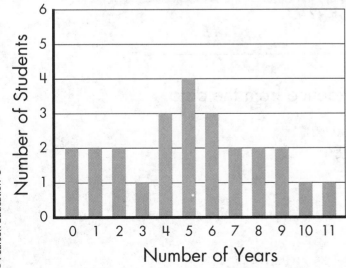

Amount of Time Fifth Graders at School #3 Have Lived in Their Homes

© Pearson Education 5

How Long Have Fifth Graders Lived in Their Homes? (page 2 of 2)

1. Compare how long fifth graders at Bartley School have lived in the homes they live in now with how long fifth graders at School #3 have lived in their homes. Write three statements about how they compare.

   a.

   b.

   c.

2. Given your comparisons of the data, which group has lived longer in their homes: fifth graders at the Bartley School or fifth graders at School #3?

   _____

   Why do you think so? Include evidence from the data.

Choosing an Experiment

Answer the following questions to plan your experiment.

1. What question will you try to answer by doing your experiment?

2. What will you be comparing?

3. What materials will you need?

4. What do you predict that the results of your experiment might be?

Planning an Experiment

1. Explain in detail the procedure for your experiment. Think about what you need to decide so that your experiment will be the same each time and you will get the information you want.

2. Share your experiment procedure with another pair of students. Do a trial run so that they can watch how you carry out your experiment. They should tell you what they found confusing and what other things they think you should include in your procedure. Make changes to your procedure in Problem 1 after hearing their feedback.

3. How will you keep track of and record your results?

Division Starter Problems

Solve each problem two ways, using the first steps listed below. Use clear and concise notation in your solutions.

NOTE Students practice flexibility in solving multiplication and division problems by finishing a solution from a given start.

SMH 38–39

1. $2,000 \div 42 =$ _____

Start by solving $840 \div 42 =$	Start by solving $40 \times 42 =$

2. $30\overline{)2,554}$

Start by solving $80 \times 30 =$	Start by solving $1,200 \div 30 =$

Teams

Solve the following problems, using clear and concise notation in your solutions.

NOTE Students solve multiplication and division problems in a story problem context.

SMH 33–34, 38–39

1. There are 112 teams in the basketball tournament. Each team has 14 players. How many basketball players are in the tournament?

2. There are 85 teams in a soccer tournament. Each team has 32 players. How many soccer players are in the tournament?

3. There are 680 students at school. They will be placed on teams of 24 for a fundraiser. How many teams will there be?

4. There are 400 students in a math bowl competition. Each school sends a team of 16 students to the competition. How many math bowl teams are in the competition?

Multiplication and Division Practice

NOTE Students practice multiplying or dividing with multiples of 10 or 100 and practice solving these problems mentally.

Try to solve all the following problems mentally. If you do not solve a problem mentally, show how you solved it.

1. $5 \times 600 =$ _____

2. $\begin{array}{r} 80 \\ \times\ 9 \\ \hline \end{array}$

3. $70 \times 60 =$ _____

4. $120 \times 12 =$ _____

5. $350 \times 20 =$ _____

6. $630 \div 9 =$ _____

7. $6\overline{)900}$

8. $75\overline{)300}$

9. $240 \div 8 =$ _____

10. $4{,}200 \div 30 =$ _____

Volunteer Mystery
Data (page 1 of 2)

> **NOTE** Students analyze data in order to develop hypotheses about the identities of different groups of volunteers.
>
> **SMH** 82

Three groups of people volunteered to help in their communities. Some of them volunteered in hospitals, in schools, or in libraries. Each person was asked how many hours he or she volunteered last year.

One group of volunteers was people who are retired. One group was mothers with young children. One group was teenagers. Look at the data and see whether you can come up with ideas about which group is which.

The Mystery Groups		
People who are retired	Teenagers	Mothers of young children

Group A: Volunteer Hours Last Year

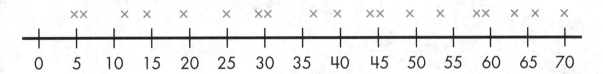

Group B: Volunteer Hours Last Year

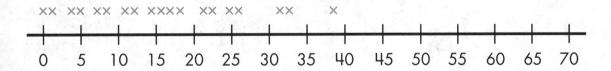

Group C: Volunteer Hours Last Year

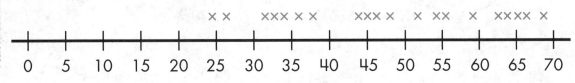

Volunteer Mystery Data (page 2 of 2)

Who do you think the groups of volunteers are? Explain what evidence in the data makes you think so.

Group A:

Group B:

Group C:

Comparing Data in Many Ways

NOTE Students compare two sets of data in many ways.

SMH **85–88**

Study the two data sets. Then complete the chart.

Girls: Balancing Time in Seconds

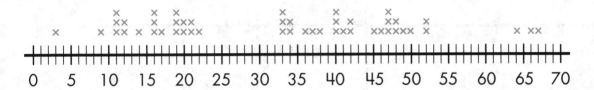

Boys: Balancing Time in Seconds

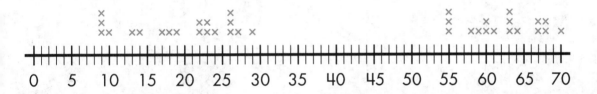

What are you comparing?	Girls	Boys	Who is better?
1. Median			
2. Highest value			
3. Top $\frac{1}{2}$ above _____ seconds			
4. Top $\frac{1}{4}$ above _____ seconds			

5. On another sheet of paper, explain which group balances better.

Ongoing Review

6. The range of the girls' balancing time is _____.

A. 70   **B.** 64   **C.** 61   **D.** 3

How Long Can You Stand on One Foot? ·   Homework

Multiplication Practice

Choose two of these problems to solve.
Solve each problem two ways.

237×76 55×168 901×49 813×28

> **NOTE** Students show their flexibility and understanding of multiplication by solving problems in two ways.
>
> **30–32**

1. Problem:

First way: Second way:

2. Problem:

First way: Second way:

Division Problems

Solve the following problems, using clear
and concise notation in your solutions.

NOTE Students practice
solving division problems.

 SMH 38–39

1. $345 \div 18 =$ _____

2. $684 \div 48 =$ _____

3. $859 \div 63 =$ _____

4. $1,572 \div 34 =$ _____

What Did You Learn from Your Experiment? (page 1 of 2)

1. What question were you trying to answer in your experiment?

2. Compare the two data sets. How do the results from your experiment compare? Write at least three things you notice.

   a.

   b.

   c.

3. What conclusions can you draw from your experiment? What do you think is the answer to your question? What evidence is there in the data to support your conclusions?

What Did You Learn from Your Experiment? (page 2 of 2)

4. If you did your experiment 100 more times, do you think your conclusions might change? Why or why not?

5. If you repeated this experiment, is there any way that you would change it or improve it?

6. On a separate sheet of paper, write a short summary of what you did. Be sure to include the following:

- What your question was
- How you would answer your question, given your data
- What the evidence is for your conclusion

You can use some of what you wrote in Problems 1, 2, and 3. Post this short summary with your representation.

Daily Practice

Matching Frequent Fliers (page 1 of 3)

NOTE Students analyze data in order to develop hypotheses about the identities of different groups of fliers.

 82

A group of students were curious to find out how many times people have flown on an airplane. They surveyed a first-grade class, a fifth-grade class, and teachers. They represented their data on bar graphs below.

Group A

How Many Times Have You Flown on an Airplane?

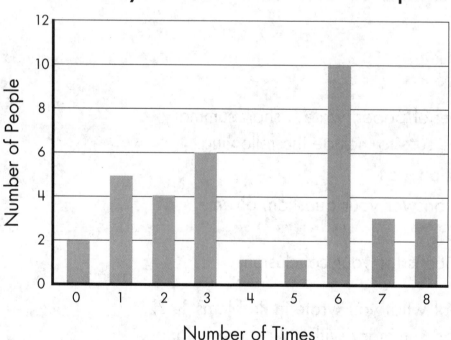

© Pearson Education **5**

Matching Frequent Fliers (page 2 of 3)

Group B

How Many Times Have You Flown on an Airplane?

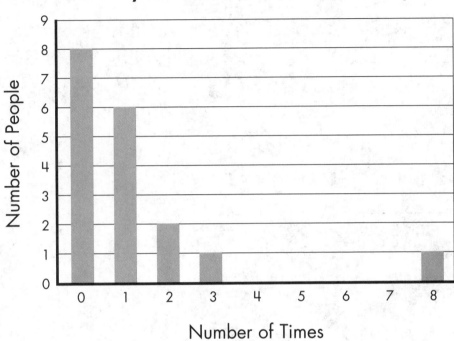

Group C

How Many Times Have You Flown on an Airplane?

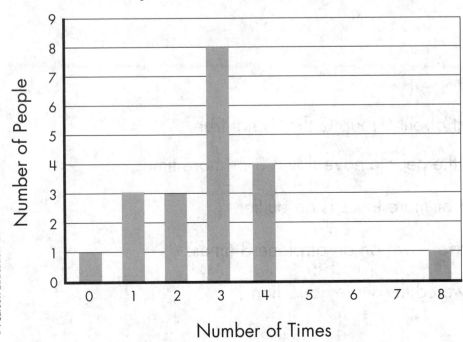

Matching Frequent Fliers (page 3 of 3)

1. Match the groups to the data sets. Write the letter for each group. Then explain what evidence in the data makes you think so.

   a. First-graders: _____

   b. Fifth-graders: _____

   c. Teachers: _____

Ongoing Review

2. Circle the statement about Group C that is not true.

   A. More than half the people have flown 3 or more times.

   B. Having flown 8 or more times is an outlier.

   C. Most people have flown on an airplane 3 times.

   D. 20 people answered the survey question.

NOTE Students compare two sets of data that are represented in bar graphs.

SMH 85–88

Who Watches More TV? (page 1 of 2)

Alicia and Charles had a disagreement about who watches more TV, adults or fifth graders. Alicia said that adults watch more TV, and Charles said that fifth graders watch more TV. They decided to find out more by doing a survey. They asked fifth graders and adults this question: About how many hours of TV do you watch each day?

They collected the data and then made a bar graph of their data. This is what the bar graph looked like:

How Many Hours a Day Do You Watch TV?

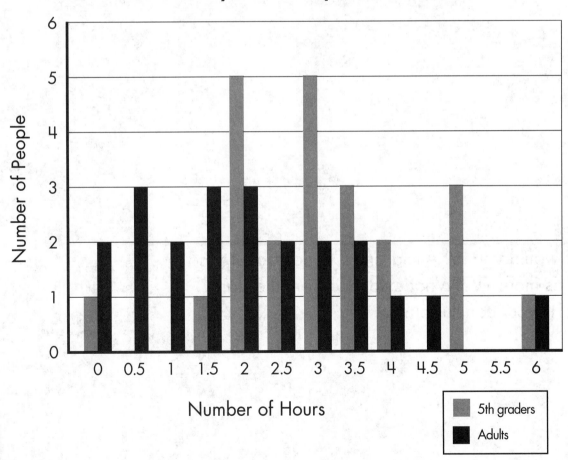

Who Watches More TV? (page 2 of 2)

1. What do you notice about how the amount of TV the fifth graders watch compares with the amount of TV the adults watch? Write three statements about what you notice.

   a.

   b.

   c.

2. What would you tell Alicia and Charles about who watches more TV? What evidence from the data supports your conclusion?

Examining the Results of Another Experiment

1. What question were your classmates trying to answer in their experiment?

2. What do you notice about the results of their experiment by looking at their representation?

3. What questions do you have about their representation, their comparisons, or their conclusions?

4. What was interesting about the results of their experiment? What did you learn from their experiment?

School Supplies

Solve the following problems, using clear and concise notation in your solutions.

NOTE Students practice solving multiplication and division problems in a story problem context.

SMH 33–34, 38–39

1. Mr. Gomez has 126 packs of pencils. Each pack has 18 pencils. How many pencils does Mr. Gomez have?

2. Ms. Tran has 580 markers. She wants to put them in bags of 24. How many bags does she need?

3. Ms. Pape has 485 books, which she is going to donate to charity. If she puts 16 in a box, how many boxes will she need for all her books?

4. Ms. Canavan has 170 packages of paintbrushes. Each package has 24 paintbrushes. How many paintbrushes does Ms. Canavan have?

School Carnival Problems

Solve each problem below. Use clear and concise notation to show your solution.

NOTE Students solve division problems in a story context.

SMH 38–39

1. The events committee is planning for a school carnival. They expect about 2,500 people to attend, and the committee needs to buy tickets. If the tickets are sold in rolls of 75, how many rolls of tickets does the events committee need to buy?

2. The concession stand needs 3,500 paper cups. If a box of cups contains 85 cups, how many boxes do they need to order?

3. Mr. Simon's class sold the most raffle tickets—871! For every 65 tickets a class sells, they earn a new book. How many books did Mr. Simon's class earn?

4. The Ferris wheel has a maximum capacity of 48 people. If it ran at full capacity all day and 1,872 rode the Ferris wheel one time each, how many times did it run?

Record of Spinner Experiment

1. How much of your spinner is colored green?

_____

2. What is the probability of landing on green?

_____

3. Predict how many times you will land on green out of 50 spins.

_____

4. Record which color you land on for each spin.

5. Record the total number of times you landed on green.

_____

Counting Puzzles

Solve the following problems, using clear and concise notation in your solutions.

NOTE Students solve multiplication and division problems in a story problem context.

SMH 30–32, 38–39

1. Mr. Jackson's class has 28 students and counts by 35s. If the first person says 35, what does the last person say?

2. Mrs. Bowker's class counts by 42s. The first person says 42, and the last person says 1,008. How many students are in Mrs. Bowker's class?

3. Ms. Hendrick's class has 26 students. They count by a certain number, and the last person says 1,560. What number are they counting by?

4. Mrs. Anderson's class has 25 students and counts by 99s. If the first person says 99, what does the last person say?

Name _____   Date _____

How Long Can You Stand on One Foot?   Daily Practice

Dollar Draw

NOTE Students review placing events on the probability line.

SMH 89, 90–91

1. Hannah won a chance to draw a gift certificate from the bowl. Find the probability that Hannah will get each lettered amount. Write the letter under the probability.

   a. $100

   b. at least $100

   c. $1,000

   d. less than $50

   e. more than $25

   f. at least $250

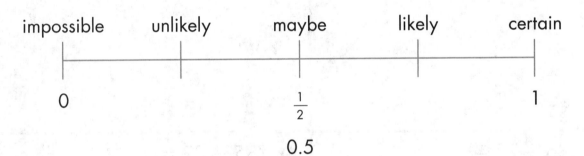

| impossible | unlikely | maybe | likely | certain |

0                            $\frac{1}{2}$ 1

0.5

Ongoing Review

2. What is the probability of drawing a gift certificate that is worth $50?

   A. $\frac{1}{8}$ **B.** $\frac{1}{4}$ **C.** $\frac{3}{8}$ **D.** $\frac{1}{2}$

Multiplying and Dividing Larger Numbers

NOTE Students practice multiplying and dividing.

SMH 33–34, 38–39

Solve the following problems, using clear and concise notation in your solutions.

1. 893
$\times$ 4

2. $647 \times 13 =$ _____

3. $1,386 \div 77 =$ _____

4. $785 \div 32 =$ _____

Race to the Top Recording Sheet

Circle the version being played: Version 1 Version 2

Round 1

A	B
START	

Round 2

A	B
START	

Round 3

A	B
START	

Round 4

A	B
START	

Round 5

A	B
START	

Round 6

A	B
START	

Field Day Prizes

The fifth grade has raised $300 to spend on prizes for Field Day. Every fifth-grade student will get a prize. Do they have enough money to buy T-shirts, water bottles, or both?

NOTE Students use multiple operations (+, −, ×, ÷) to solve a problem in a story context.

Prices	Fifth-Grade Class Sizes	
T-shirts:	Mr. A's class:	19 students
12 for $50	Ms. Q's class:	23 students
	Mrs. B's class:	18 students
Water Bottles:	Mr. R's class:	21 students
18 for $30.99	Ms. S's class:	20 students

Name _____ Date _____

How Long Can You Stand on One Foot?   Homework

Spin to Win

The fifth-grade booth at the school
fair features this wheel.

NOTE Students compare the
actual results of spinning a
spinner with expected results.

SMH 90–91

$\frac{1}{3}$ **Probability of
Winning a Teddy Bear!**

Sorry

Sorry

1. How many times would you expect
   to get a teddy bear out of 60 spins? _____

2. The table shows the last 60 spins of the wheel.
   Compare the actual results with the expected results.

Teddy Bear	22
Sorry	38
Total	60

3. How would you expect the results of the next 60 spins
   to compare with these results?

Ongoing Review

4. When someone spins the spinner, what is the
   probability of the spinner landing on "Sorry?"

   A. $\frac{3}{4}$ **B.** $\frac{2}{3}$ **C.** $\frac{1}{2}$ **D.** $\frac{1}{3}$

New Race to the Top Directions (page 1 of 2) WRITING

Make new rules for Race to the Top: Version 2 to make it a fair game. The following are the rules you cannot change:

- You must use the Version 2 spinner, and you cannot change it.
- Players must flip a coin to determine who gets to choose which player they will be.
- Players A and B must stay the same throughout all 6 rounds.

1. Write out the directions below to your new version of the game that uses the Race to the Top: Version 2 spinner.

New Race to the Top
Directions (page 2 of 2) ✏️WRITING

2. Do you think this game is fair now? Explain why you
think it is fair or, if you are not sure, why you are
not sure.

Name _____ Date _____

How Long Can You Stand on One Foot?   Daily Practice

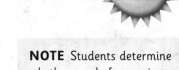

Fair or Unfair?

The spinner is $\frac{3}{4}$ shaded. Suppose that players take turns spinning it. Decide whether each game is fair and tell why.

NOTE Students determine whether a rule for a spinner game is fair or unfair.

SMH 92

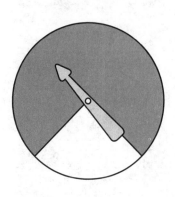

1. Game 1: On his or her turn, a player scores a point for spinning white, no points for shaded. The first person to 10 points is the winner.

2. Game 2: For each turn, Player 1 gets 3 points for white and Player 2 gets 1 point for shaded. The first person to 12 points is the winner.

Ongoing Review

3. Suppose that the spinner is spun 100 times. Which is the most likely number of spins to land on blue?

   A. 25   **B.** 50   **C.** 75   **D.** 90

On Sale!

Solve the following problems, using clear and concise notation in your solutions.

NOTE Students solve multistep multiplication and division problems in story contexts.

SMH 30–32, 38–39

1. A magazine is offering a special subscription rate of $29 per year for 12 issues. The regular price for the magazine is $3.99 per issue. If you subscribe at the special rate, how much money will you save?

2. Mrs. Nelson needs to order 348 jars of paint for her art classroom. This week a box of 12 jars of paint is on sale at the art store for $16.00 per box. How many boxes does Mrs. Nelson need to buy? How much will the paint cost?

3. Which is the better buy?

   a 9-pack of juice boxes
   for $3.59

   or

   a case of 24 juice boxes
   for $11.95

4. Toshiki's goal is to work out at the gym 15 days each month. Which gym should he join?

   Membership at Gym A:
   $39 per month

   or

   Membership at Gym B:
   $2.75 per visit

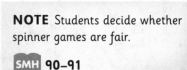

Toys in the Attic

Todd found an old spinner game in the attic. He could not find the rules, so he tried to make up his own. He wrote three different versions.

NOTE Students decide whether spinner games are fair.

SMH 90–91

1. For each version, decide whether the game is fair. Explain your reasoning on another sheet of paper.

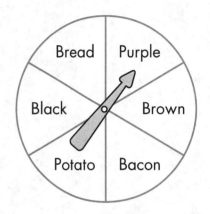

Version A

Player A gets 1 point if the spinner lands on a 5-letter word.

Player B gets 1 point if the spinner lands on a 6-letter word.

Version B

Player A gets 1 point if the spinner lands on a color.

Player B gets 1 point if the spinner lands on a food.

Version C

Player A gets 1 point if the spinner lands on a word that begins with "b."

Player B gets 1 point if the spinner lands on a word that begins with "p."

2. Complete the following rule so the game is fair.
   Player A gets a point if the spinner lands on a word containing the letter _____; otherwise Player B gets a point.